Knitting Without Tears

Knitting
Without Tears

BASIC TECHNIQUES AND EASY-TO-FOLLOW
DIRECTIONS FOR GARMENTS TO FIT ALL SIZES

by Elizabeth Zimmermann

Charles Scribner's Sons, New York

ACKNOWLEDGMENTS to my husband, for his patience and for his knowledge of the English language; to Tom, for photography; to Elinor Parker, my Editor, for everything.

11 13 15 17 19 Q/P 20 18 16 14 12

Printed in the United States of America
SBN 684-106892 (Cloth)
SBN 684-13505-1 (Paper)

Library of Congress Catalog Card Number 70–140776

Contents

Dedicated to Barbara Abbey and Barbara Walker,

with affection and respect.

Knitting Without Tears

Chapter 1

The Opinionated Knitter

MOST people have an obsession; mine is knitting.

Your hobby may be pie-baking, playing the piano, or potbelly-stove collecting, and you can sympathize with my enthusiasm, having an obsession of your own. Will you forgive my single-mindedness, and my tendency to see knitting in everything?

Carvings and sculpture remind me only of Aran and other textured designs; when I see a beautiful print my first thought is how it would adapt to color pattern knitting; confronted by a new fashion, I immediately start drawing in the air with my forefinger to see if it would suit itself to knitting, and if so, how—which way the grain should run, if the shape could be knitted in, and what stitch would be most effective.

So please bear with me, and put up with my opinionated, nay, sometimes cantankerous attitude. I feel strongly about knitting.

What follows is an attempt to explain some of the ideas that come while designing knitted garments, and during the pleasant hours spent working on the plain straight pieces.

1

I am taking it for granted that you are already familiar with the rudiments of the craft.

Properly practiced, knitting soothes the troubled spirit, and it doesn't hurt the untroubled spirit either.

When I say properly practiced, I mean executed in a relaxed manner, without anxiety, strain, or tension, but with confidence, inventiveness, pleasure, and ultimate pride.

If you hate to knit, why, bless you, don't; follow your secret heart and take up something else. But if you start out knitting with enjoyment, you will probably continue in this pleasant path.

Consider the agreeable material and tools. (I admit to a rooted preference for wool.)

WOOL

Soft wool from the simple silly sheep can be as fine as a cobweb, tough and strong as string, or light and soft as down. There are scientific reasons why wool is the best material for knitting, and into these I will not go. I only know that it is warm, beautiful, and durable. Woolen socks never become cold and clammy, however wet. A woolen sweater is so water-resistant that when dropped overboard it floats long enough to give you ample time to rescue it. The surface on caps and mittens made of wool repels all but the most persistent of downpours. I have in mind a particularly beautiful cap made of the finest wool and angora at seven stitches to the inch in the lovely designs of Bohus in Sweden. It has been worn for two seasons by a dedicated ski-teacher in all manner of blizzards and dirty weather, and she swears that it is the warmest and driest hat she has—snow perches on it but does not penetrate.

For people allergic to wool, one's heart can only bleed. Synthetics are a marvelous substitute, but a substitute is all they are. The allergic must be grateful that they didn't live in the Dark Ages of fifty years ago when one kept warm in winter with wool, or froze to death in linen and cotton. Of course, some avoided pleurisy by swathing themselves in sables.

It is true that a synthetic sweater can be washed and dried in machines, but to me this rather reduces it to the level of a sweatshirt. Washing a real sweater is akin to bathing a baby, and brings the same satisfaction of producing a clean, pretty, sweet-smelling creature—very rewarding.

There is a persuasive old wives' tale about one reason why wool shrinks. It goes, "Never wind your wool into a tight hard ball, as this will make it stretched and taut. You knit it up into a sweater. Then it gets dirty and you wash it. The wool, encouraged by the dampness, goes back to its original unstretched state, with the result that the whole sweater shrinks." Think it over.

"Ply" is a frequently misunderstood concept. It has nothing to do with the thickness of yarn, except in a relative way, and everything to do with its construction.

A ply is a strand of wool. Two, three, four, or more strands are twisted together to make 2-ply, 3-ply, 4-ply, or many-plied wool. Since the strands or plies can be of any thickness, it is clear that the thickness of wool does not depend on the *number* of plies but on the *thickness* of the individual ply. I have used 9-ply wool which was no thicker than 4-ply knitting worsted, and I'm sure all are familiar with 2-ply wool so heavy and bulky that it knits up at 2½ stitches to 1 inch.

So when buying wool be guided by the recommended GAUGE rather than by the number of plies, and compare this recommended GAUGE with the GAUGE specified in your knitting instructions.

When wondering how much wool to buy, ask the saleslady. She knows by experience. If she doesn't know and

3

isn't interested, go to another store. In fact, start off by going to the best specialty yarn shop or good department store that you can find. It is not wise to shop around for cheap wool unless you are very experienced, or are willing to risk spending hours of work on an object that will shrink, fade, or run. A well-made sweater, knitted with good will and good wool, is beyond price; why try to save a dollar on the material?

Consult the nice expert in the wool shop, and if she doesn't suggest taking an extra skein as insurance against running short, take one anyway. Find out the time limit on returns and exchanges, and mark this on your sales slip. And keep the sales slip with the wool, OK? The saleslady will then love you. Even if you never get around to returning the extra skein, think what a disaster it would be to run short, and to fail to match the dye lot. Anyway, extra skeins are always useful for socks, caps, mittens, color patterns, or stripes.

If you prefer to economize and love to knit, make your sweaters with very fine wool and many stitches. A thin sweater weighs much less than a great heavy one, and, broadly speaking, wool sells by weight. Fine knitting gives you many more hours of your favorite hobby before you have to sally forth and make another capital investment.

Discrepancies will occur between dye lots; even with white, even with black. Never start a project without sufficient wool to finish it.

But on a rainy winter's night who can resist three or four skeins of wool, pleading to be made into a sweater? "I'll go to the wool shop first thing, and match the wool." Oh dear. Famous last words.

Well, there are several remedies.

If you can find an almost perfect match, the two shades may be successfully blended by working them in alternate rows for an inch or two.

Seams will also help to hide the slight color difference of a close match. You may make one or both sleeves of the new color, which will fool the eye.

If the match is Not Good At All, you can be glad you are making a Zimmermann sweater (I hope you are). Several of these start at the bottom on sleeves and body; the three pieces are united at the underarm, and the shoulders or yoke are worked last. This offers endless opportunities for using up odd wools. Few people embark on a new sweater overnight without material to get them at least to the underarm. So when the wool runs out decide that you had decided on a sweater with a contrasting yoke anyway. Eureka. If you are determined to have a one-color garment, intersperse a few purl rounds where the dye lot change occurs. This is enough to fool most eyes, even if it never fools yours—you know too much. You can put in a small pretty color pattern at the point of change, which may please you so much that you may decide to continue with different color patterns up to the neck. This is one way of achieving a "famous masterpiece of taste and imagination." Save a few yards of the original color for one of the last patterns, and the whole thing will look as if it had been planned.

NEEDLES

Needles are made of so many materials that you can go dizzy taking your pick. Years ago you had your choice of wood, bone, steel, or luxurious tortoiseshell and ivory. The contemporary ones are usually of metal or plastic, and are firm or flexible respectively.

The U.S., for some reason, employs different size numbers from those in Europe, which are measured in millimeters. A needle gauge is a very useful thing to own, although it and the needles may vary infinitesimally, which sometimes leads to confusion. Occasionally one comes upon a mature needle gauge in which the holes have actually become enlarged through constant use, or by the forcing through of too large needles.

This all points to the admonition not to take needle sizes too seriously, especially if you tend to knit loosely.

Tight knitters lead a hard and anxious life. They grab needles and wool so tightly that great strain is put upon their hand muscles, nay, arm, shoulder, and even neck muscles in extreme cases. They must let go of everything from time to time, just to rest, and then resume knitting, with what looks like a careworn expression, although they neither admit, nor, in most cases, believe this. The tight little stitches they make must be forced along their (right) needle, and more tight little stitches force up along their (left) needle, to be squeezed in their turn. The resulting fabric, in knitting worsted, with #8 needles, can have a GAUGE of five stitches to one inch, because of the great tightness. The identical GAUGE may be easily and calmly achieved by a loose knitter on, say, #5 needles.

If you are a beginning knitter, don't try to knit tightly in order to make your work look neat.

If you are a habitually tight knitter, try to kick the habit.

Loose knitting tends to make your stitches look somewhat uneven, but what of it? Are you trying to reproduce a boughten machine-made sweater? Besides, it is surprising what blocking and a few washings will do to uneven knitting.

I used to think that people in the Olden Days were marvelously even knitters, because all really ancient sweaters are so smooth and regular. Now I realize that they probably knitted just as I do, rather erratically, and that it is Time, the Great Leveller, which has wrought the change—Time, and many washings.

Don't fuss too much about one size in needles; it is

GAUGE that is important, and this does not invariably depend on needle size. If you want to make a sock and can find only three #2 needles, add unto them a #1 or a #3; it will make very little difference if you are a loose knitter. I have, on a bet, made a sock on four different-sized needles without ill effect. One tends to give one's fingers too little credit for their innate good sense. *They* feel when a too-thick needle has arrived on the scene, and will tighten up a tad. Confronted by a really skinny needle, they will help the little thing along by loosening up, and no harm done. One is in this knitting pastime for pleasure, not for toil, anxiety, and doubt, so don't WORRY. If you are a tight knitter by chance instead of by choice, practice knitting loosely, and it may change your life.

Different needle materials are:

Wood

Very useful in the larger sizes—say #10 to #15. Well-worn wooden needles can become well loved. Their benevolent clack is soothing, and brings back the feeling of childhood. New needles, not mellowed, may be broken in with sandpaper or steel wool, and light applications of paste wax or linseed oil, but the best finish is attained by years of use, preferably with natural oiled wool.

Bone

These have become quite rare, and should be treasured. Sandpaper helps them too.

Steel

The original clicking needles, which come in small sizes, for socks and lace. They tend to rust, so get out the steel wool, and oil them lightly before putting them away.

Tortoiseshell and Ivory
Museum pieces. Cherish them.

Celluloid
The famous old fire hazard, but why sit so close to the candle? Extremely brittle; not to be sat upon.

Aluminum
Good rigid needles. If the outer coating has worn off, watch out when using them with natural oily wool (sometimes called "boot wool"). The lanolin in the wool causes the metal to blacken, and this will come off on your knitting. No great tragedy, as it washes out quite easily, but rather unsettling. A #6 aluminum needle has been known to furnish an excellent emergency shearpin for an outboard motor. It once saved us seven miles of paddling. Then I had to spend hours re-pointing the needle on rocks, having nobly, but foolishly, offered the business end instead of the knob end for sacrifice.

Plastic-Coated Metal
An excellent rigid needle. Bends when sat upon, but is easily bent back.

Plastic or Nylon
Splendid for those who like flexible needles.

Walrus Tusk
It is pure boasting to mention these. I own a few sets, and use them reverently. They are as gently curved as the tusk from which they sprang.

That takes care of straight needles. Find out which kind you prefer. Some have blunter points than others and these are fine for loose knitters, while tight knitters are more com-

8

fortable with relatively sharper points. They come in sets of two, with knobs, for working back and forth, or in sets of four, without knobs, for circular knitting. In Europe they come in fives, as there the sock itself is on four needles, with the fifth one used for knitting. Emergency knobs for double-pointed needles may be made from tightly wound rubber bands, or from those rubber needle guards which are never to be found when wanted. Dorothy Case links her needle guards with wool; then they can both get lost together.

To sharpen the knob end of a wood or plastic needle, try the pencil sharpener and sandpaper.

Circular Needles

Circular needles are my particular pets. They have changed enormously since my youth, when they were formed of a piece of wire with knitting-needle-like points. The joint between wire and point was far from strong, but it rarely broke apart so that you could honorably throw the thing away. One little strand of wire would come loose, and catch on every single stitch brought up to the left point to be knitted. You could resourcefully reverse the whole piece of knitting, so that the stitches were pulled over the faulty end on the right side, which didn't seem to matter, but then the other end would soon start fraying. I'm pretty sure that this is the reason for the rooted dislike of circular knitting evinced by some of my generation; I can think of no other cause. Younger people are more open-minded and love circular knitting, but suffer under a great paucity of directions for the technique. This gap I am valiantly trying to fill.

Circular needles are now beyond reproach, as far as durability goes. Different versions vary considerably. You can find them in all-nylon, or in nylon with metal points, and in a great variety of lengths. I use the 16″ and the 24″ lengths only; the extra 3″ on a 27″ length just seem to get

9

in my way. But even a 36″ length is happily used by some.

I like the 16″ length for sleeves, caps, and children's sweaters. The 24″ length will take care of any sweater, skirt or shawl that I care to make. When I tell you that once in the latter stages of an ambitious project I had well over a thousand stitches on a 24″ needle, would you believe me? It's true, and I had no trouble, except that the beginning of the round became lost in the scrimmage, and I found it wise to mark the place with a generous piece of scarlet wool. Marooned on a lonely island once, for two weeks, I managed 320 stitches on a 16″ needle, but this was no fun.

There are in existence 11″, and even stunted little 9″ circular needles, but I mention them chiefly for academic reasons. I will, on occasion, use an 11″ needle for making Norwegian mittens in color patterns. Working color patterns on four needles is apt to cause tension trouble when one changes from one needle to the next, and a circular needle eliminates this. But a needle so short has of necessity very short ends to grasp, and to knit holding the working end of the needle in thumb and forefinger can be tiring and disagreeable.

See to it that the ends of any circular needle you buy are long enough to hold comfortably—at least 3½″ on the 16″ length, and up to 5″ on the 24″ length. Try various kinds of needles to see which kind you prefer, and build up a collection of the sizes and lengths most often used. I like to have 16″ needles in pairs, so that I can work on two sleeves at once if I feel like it. All-nylon needles have slightly flexible ends, especially in the smaller sizes, and I rather like them for color patterns. However, when working any kind of Aran pattern or cable, I prefer the rigid metal ends, which enable one to dig into recalcitrant stitches on occasion.

It is perfectly possible and—in airplane seats, for instance

10

—desirable, to use a circular needle for working back and forth. And one runs no risk of losing a needle.

OTHER TOOLS

Useful adjuncts for knitting are a yardstick or tape measure, scissors, needle gauge, and two large wool needles, one blunt, one sharp. Tapestry needles are all right for fine wool, but they cause knitting worsted and the heavier wools to bulk up behind the eye, and to have to be dragged through the fabric. So hunt up some larger ones. If you can find some of those markers like small safety pins with no eyes, take several cards. A smallish crochet hook will be useful on occasion. Really, all you need to become a good knitter are wool, needles, hands, and slightly below-average intelligence. Of course superior intelligence, such as yours and mine, is an advantage.

FABRIC AND TEXTURE

Let us proceed to fabric and texture. The hundreds, even thousands, of usable stitch patterns available to knitters have been well recorded elsewhere. I shall not attempt to go into the subject, but will content myself by describing the most usual plain ones, and the particular qualities which make them suitable for various purposes.

The most obvious one to start with is *stocking stitch*. It is not always the easiest, but it is the most often used. It may be executed in two ways; either by working back and forth on two needles in alternate rows of knit and purl, or by knitting around continuously on a circular needle, or on four needles, to form a circular seamless fabric. I use it a great deal for its severe simplicity. It allows the construction of the garment to be more clearly visible, with all its inventive increasing, decreasing, and shaping. Since I am

11

most interested in the construction details of knitted garments, this appeals to me strongly. However, my designs may be executed in any stitch pattern that takes your fancy, as long as you reproduce the shaping correctly.

Stocking stitch likes to curl; towards you from the top and the bottom; away from you at the sides. This phenomenon occurs because each stitch is infinitesimally shorter on the front than on the back, and infinitesimally wider horizontally. Therefore the fabric curls, as a piece of bread curls when the upper surface dries, and therefore shrinks. Consequently the borders of anything made in this stitch should be made in a stitch that will not curl, such as garter stitch, seed stitch, or ribbing. The borders of a stocking stitch cardigan need not be integral with the main body of the knitting—they may be added afterwards, either being sewn on, or, better still, knitted up (picked up), and worked vertically. This will enable you to control the relative lengths of body and border, and combat the regrettable tendency of fronts to droop, frill out, or, on the other hand, pucker.

All-purl is the reverse of stocking stitch, and is sometimes used for sweaters, giving them rather an inside-out look. It is excellent as a background for patterns such as cables, or the intricate convolutions of Aran (fisherman) sweaterpatterns. One row of purl on a stocking stitch fabric stands out sharply, and makes an excellent turn line for a hem. Two, three, or even more rows of purl make a splendidly heavy horizontal welt or ridge. Purling will not do this for you when worked vertically; it will turn its back on you and recede. However, a vertical line of knit stitches on a purl fabric will stand out nobly.

Garter stitch is the easiest of all stitches, and one of the best looking. It is achieved simply by working back and forth in all-knit. (In circular knitting you would have to

12

knit one round and purl one round alternately—not worth it.) Each knit stitch, as you form it, makes a smooth V towards you, and a knobby little pearl on the reverse side. Thus by knitting back and forth on alternate sides, the smooth and the knobby rows will succeed each other, each one paired with its own knobby and smooth rows on the other side. (In stocking stitch the Vs are all on one side; the knobs all on the other.) Garter stitch has no right or wrong side—both sides are the same. Tied in with the principle of curl and counter-curl is the fact that the edges will never curl. This makes the stitch particularly suitable for blankets, afghans, and, above all, baby clothes. How often one wishes that one could, in an emergency, turn a baby's sweater inside out. With a garter stitch sweater one can. Always finish garments made in this stitch extra-neatly on the inside—one never knows.

1. KNIT STITCH (front)

2. KNIT STITCH (back)

Garter stitch has a very pronounced grain, caused by the ridges of its construction, and it is fascinating to employ it running both horizontally and vertically, so that it catches light and shadow differently. Its interesting texture is thus accentuated.

Ribbing, consisting of alternating vertical lines of stocking stitch and reverse stocking stitch, is very useful in its simpler forms. It yields a splendidly elastic lower border for sweaters, and the best socks are made in all-rib, so that they cling to the ankles and don't draggle. Sweaters made in all-rib tend to adhere inordinately, so if you want to wear a ribbed sweater and retain your dignity, be sure that it has many more stitches than you would think possible.

If you twist all the stitches in ribbing—that is, knit into the back of the K stitches and purl into the back of the P stitches—you will attain a very elastic ribbing, indeed, and a very elegant one. Or you may knit into the back of the

13

K stitches only. When working back and forth on two needles this yields a certain elasticity, and gives the knit rib a rather pleasant irregularity, as it is twisted only every second row. Practically all my ribbing is worked on circular needles, and therefore my knit stitches can be *all* twisted, which is very effective, and a nice bonus for the circular knitter. Such facts back up my predilection for making knitting as diverting and pleasant as possible, but this is a very subjective matter. Some knitters get an enormous charge out of employing the most difficult methods and performing the job perfectly. They will obviously want to twist both the knit and the purl stitches in ribbing, and have my blessing. At the other end of the scale, there are those who are made extremely nervous by working into the back of any stitch whatsoever, and they should eschew it, by all means. It is not an essential part of knitting.

Ribbing may be as elaborately ornamented with various cables and fancy stitches as you please, and is the foundation of the lovely Aran fisherman patterns from Ireland. As Aran stitches are basically a form of ribbing, it is unnecessary to put ribbing at the border of an Aran sweater, since it will not curl anyway. To hold in the lower edges and cuffs, you may arrange to have fewer purl stitches between the patterns for the first few inches, and then increase up to the required amount for the main body of the sweater. Increasing by "Make 1" (see p. 27) is practically invisible in purling.

Many of the original Irish sweaters have a border of a completely different series of patterns from the main body of the sweater—usually "Tree of Life" or small cables.

TECHNIQUES

Knitting Techniques is a very grand phrase, and a deceptive one, for there are only two techniques—right-handed

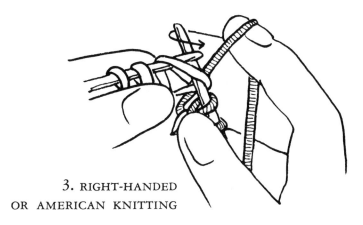

3. RIGHT-HANDED
OR AMERICAN KNITTING

knitting and left-handed knitting, i.e., working with the wool in the right hand or in the left hand.*

Right-handed knitters, who throw their wool with their right hand, are often said to knit the "English" or the "American" way. I believe that this method originated when knitting was worked on extremely long needles (or "wires"). The right needle had its end tucked into the belt, or into a sheath attached to the belt. The business ends of both needles were held with the left hand, which enabled the free right hand to feed the wool to be knitted at surprising speed. Vestiges of this technique are occasionally noticed in some knitters, who hold the end of one of our contemporary 14" needles tucked under the right arm. Most knitters who work this way need three movements for each stitch: needle in, wrap wool around it, pull stitch through.

Left-handed knitters are usually those with a Continental European background (although I have noticed some Europeans knitting right-handed). They hold the wool over their

* For some reason the right-handers scorn the left-handers, causing the poor left-handers to labor, with great humility, under a quite unsubstantiated feeling of inferiority. It is my belief—and please feel free to disagree with me—that because right-handed knitting is prevalent in the British Isles, it is considered more elegant. Those with Anglo-Saxon names, such as mine originally was, tend rather regrettably to look down on others. Why?

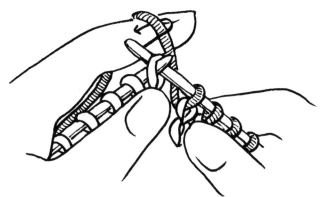

4. LEFT-HANDED, OR GERMAN KNITTING

left forefinger, and hook each stitch through with the right
needle. Two movements—needle in: wool through and off.
Some hold their left forefinger high; some leave it low and
relaxed. Some wind the wool several times around their
left forefinger, and release it, a loop at a time. Some make
a veritable cat's cradle around several fingers, apparently
to regulate tension. But they are all left-handed knitters,
and on an average far outdistance the right-handed knitters
for speed.

I am myself a left-handed knitter, but not by birth. At
my mother's knee I was taught right-handed—slip, over,
under, off—and thus did I achieve my first childish kettle-
holders and useful navy-blue mats for putting under ink-
wells. In the course of time, as was then the custom, our
family fell under the sway of governesses; a teaching-in-the-
schoolroom governess for the older children, and a Swiss
nursery-governess for the baby. Need I say that the English
and the Swiss governesses knitted the right-handed and the
left-handed way respectively? Need I also say that I was
fascinated by the Swiss knitting, and attempted to copy it?
Of course I needn't. But you may be forgiven for disbeliev-
ing the result. The year was 1920, and the English governess,
noticing my unorthodox way of knitting, uncompromising-
ly forbade the practice of anything as despicable as the

16

German way of knitting. The obvious upshot was that I used to practice secretly, soon became addicted, and, after merciful release from this particular governess, came out into the open with my foreign habit, and have never looked back.

One advantage of this episode is that my method of holding the wool is a little unusual, as I was self-taught. My left forefinger is held low, and is also used for holding the left needle. The wool runs over it and under the other three fingers, which manage quite happily to regulate the tension. I knit only fairly fast—45 to a top speed of 51 stitches a minute—but am quite content with this, as my hands and arms remain loose and comfortable. I have not forgotten the right-handed method, and find it useful on occasion, as you shall see.

So, please, knit the way you prefer, and cultivate a nodding acquaintance with the other way, as a second string to your bow.

One word to left-handed knitters: in purling, some of you hook the wool through the stitch the easiest way; down and over the top of it. This makes the stitch come at you back to front the next time you work it, so that you must knit out of the back of it. Most of you know enough to compensate for this, and work out of the stitch logically, whichever way it presents itself to you, but it poses a problem to some knitters. It is really worthwhile to train yourself, when purling, to come at the thread from below, and then up in front of it, and down. Considered as a loop, the right side of the stitch should always be in front of the needle when you come to work it.

5. ONE WAY TO PURL

Actually, there is no wrong way to knit, although there is one way which is nearly wrong. I mean Backwards, or Looking-Glass Knitting. It is not wrong in effect, as its proponents—or shall we say victims?—turn out perfectly

6. A BETTER WAY TO PURL

creditable garments. But they work in a void of noncom-munication, cut off from all run-of-the-mill knitters and nearly all knitting instructions.

Those who really knit left-handed, or backwards, take their stitches from the right needle on to the left, instead of the other way around. They appear to believe that because they write left-handed they should knit left-handed too. (How they can operate a typewriter, or a sewing machine, or a telephone has always baffled me.) They forget that left-handed writing is legible to everybody, while watching backwards knitting leaves the observer feeling as if she had to decide whether to put the clock backwards or forwards in Spring, unaided by mnemonics, and at the same time patting her head with one hand and rubbing her stomach with the other, and then reversing matters.

In point of fact, somebody with more agility in the left hand should take to German knitting as a duck to water, for in this method the left hand has much more to do. But the left-handed, finding it awkward to learn to knit, seem to think that this comes from their own left-handedness, and not from the natural awkwardness we all experience when learning a new skill.

To be truthful, I must admit to having taught myself to knit backwards in one of my efforts to avoid my *bête noire,* purl. No purpose can be served by pretending that purling is too easy the "German" way. I argued—rightly, I think—that with two-needle knitting, working across in knit and back in looking-glass knit, one could achieve stocking-stitch without the nuisance of purling. One could. But the game wasn't worth the candle, except as a feat of skill. I soon turned to circular knitting as a solution to my inborn dislike of purling.

Why do so many of us object to purling? Is it because as children we are taught to knit first, and are then presented

18

with purling as the second and more difficult step? Who knows? Who is willing to take a little innocent child and teach it to purl first? You must admit it's the trickier of the two.

Of course, purling is not so bad for right-handed knitters; in fact I know several who knit with the wool in the left hand and purl with it in the right hand. However, this doesn't save them when it comes to pattern stitches involving knit *and* purl. This is a vale of tears and no mistake. Things are not perfect, and we wouldn't appreciate it if they were.

DETAILS

Casting-on

It is important to cast on quite loosely. If you find this difficult, use a very large needle, or even two needles held together.

Do not expect a tight casting-on to "hold in" the bottom of a garment. It will only give you a horrid, tight, unyielding edge, which may wear out before its time.

There are two basic methods of casting-on, both good.

1. The first consists of making a loop over the right needle, leaving a long tail of wool, which often turns out

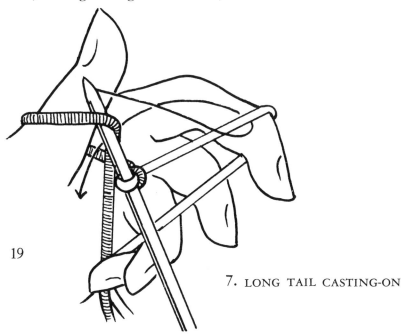

19

7. LONG TAIL CASTING-ON

8. BASIC LOOP

9. KNITTING-ON

10. LOOP CASTING-ON

11. TWISTED LOOP
CASTING-ON

to be too short (infuriating), or too long (wasteful, and therefore also infuriating). Loop on the stitches, using both ends of wool, or knit them through loops formed on the left thumb. The result is the same. When the tail turns out to be too short, with perhaps just a few stitches to go, take another length of wool, and cast on one stitch with the old and the new wools together, finishing with the new wool. The ends are darned in later, and will never show. Better still, you can cast on using the ends from two balls of wool.

2. The knitting-on method is really the best way to cast on. With it you knit one stitch into your basic loop (no long tail to bother with—3"- 4" is enough), and put this new stitch also on the left needle. Now don't knit *into* it, the way some of us were taught as children, but *between* it and the first stitch, and put this third stitch also on the needle. Knit *between* the third stitch and the second, then *between* the fourth and the third, and so on, always putting the new-made stitch on the left needle. You are making a fine strong flexible border. It may seem tight at first, but a good pull will stretch it into shape. This casting-on, when completed, looks equally well on both sides; a great blessing on any border to be turned up or down. With all the advantages of this method, why do I stubbornly continue to use the long-tail method? I don't know.

3. There are two more peripheral ways of casting-on, the first of which is a series of backward loops over the right needle, useful only in some types of buttonholes, and in emergencies. If you can train yourself to *twist the loop* before putting it on the needle, it is a great improvement, and may perhaps find yourself using this version frequently.

4. Then there is "Invisible Casting-on" which can prove very useful when joining the end of something to its beginning, or, as I have only recently discovered, when you want to make a sweater from the neck down (*not* my favorite

20

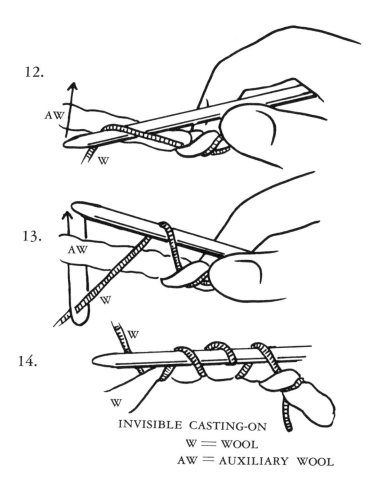

12.

13.

14.

INVISIBLE CASTING-ON
W = WOOL
AW = AUXILIARY WOOL

design) with apparently totally seamless underarms. This casting-on consists of loops formed around a needle and a contrasting auxiliary wool. When the Auxiliary Wool is later removed you will find a row of stitches ready to be picked up, or woven, as the case may be. This is how to do it: Knot wool (W) with a piece of Auxiliary Wool (AW). Place the needle in the right hand between W and AW and hold wools taut in left hand with AW above. *With needle in right hand, come down in *front* of AW, behind and under W, and up. With needle come down *behind* AW, behind and under W, and up. Repeat from * until the desired number of stitches has been formed by loops over the needle, simply ducking down alternately in front of and

21

behind AW, and fishing up a loop of W each time. Keep AW parallel to, and under, needle. For the first row, knit into the loops on the needle as you would into cast-on stitches. Pulling out AW when knitting is completed will release the loops to be picked up and knitted down, or woven. I am often asked which is the "right side" of casting-on. My answer is: the right side is the one which looks best to *you*. *I* prefer the side which looks like embroidered outline-stitch.

Casting-off

1. This has been limited to only one method. Work two stitches, pull the first one over the second, work a third stitch, pull the second one over it, work a fourth stitch, pull the third one over it, and so on. The main trick is to keep an optimum tension; not so tight that it binds, and not so loose that it looks sloppy; in fact, a happy medium, best attained through practice and experience. Remember to work the stitches as they present themselves, as the French so cleverly put it, "comme ils se présentent," knitting the knit stitches and purling the purl ones. To make a neat final corner when casting off, work the last two stitches together.

I always swore I would invent a casting-off method when I had time, and one day, a couple of years ago, I did. It has a disadvantage, as it cannot be ripped, but must be taken out, stitch by stitch, if necessary. But there is an advantage too; it doesn't look like casting-off. Do you have that feeling about casting-off? That it often looks rather homemade? Well this Sewn Casting-off really looks more like casting-on. It is very useful for finishing garter stitch, and in the case of stocking stitch causes it to curl less stubbornly. (Not advisable for ribbing.) I like to use it on enigmatic garments with which I try to puzzle other knitters: "Guess how this was made." The first thing they look for is where I cast off, and if they can't find it they are very often flummoxed.

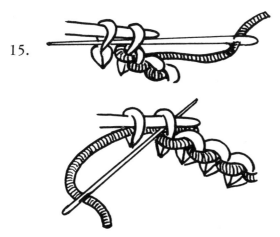

15.

16. SEWN CASTING-OFF

Sewn Casting-off

2. This is the method. Break wool, leaving a good working length, which is threaded through a blunt wool needle. Holding the work in the left hand, *put this needle through the first two stitches as if to purl, from right to left. Pull wool through. Put needle back through the first stitch as if to knit, from left to right. Pull wool through. Slip first stitch off needle. Repeat from *; two steps forward, one step back, two steps forward, one step back. Do not pull the wool too tight, although there is little danger of this.

A good way to cast off garter stitch is on the right side in purl. This has a way of curling over on the right side, and of flattening itself on the wrong side.

"Casting-on casting-off" has just sprung into being, fully fledged. Although I will claim invention of this technique, I will not claim its original invention. Someone else may have thought of it, and forgotten it again. All I assert is that I have never seen it or heard of it before.

This casting-off is a facsimile of casting-on.

Cast-off in Outline Stitch

3. If you have ever taken out the absolute lowest row of casting-on—the part that looks like embroidered outline stitch—you may have noticed that it *is* in reality very much like outline stitch, being a species of overcasting which links

23

the stitches by pairs. When it is removed it reveals a row of stitch loops, which, in the case of stocking stitch and garter stitch, may be picked up and used for knitting down in the opposite direction.

Why not finish your work with a similar row of outline stitch?

Why not, indeed.

Break the wool, and thread it through a good blunt needle. Hold the work with the right side towards you, with the wool coming from the left end. Work from Left to Right. *Keeping the working wool above, go into the second stitch from the front, and into the first stitch from the back. Pull the wool through both stitches. Slip the first stitch off the needle. Repeat from *, keeping the tension fairly loose; it may be tightened later.

17. CASTING-ON CASTING-OFF

I hope you will soon become sufficiently confident to take the stitches off the knitting needle.

Cast-off Variation

4. What I just said about somebody having invented a stitch and then forgotten it again has come back home to roost. Barbara Walker has reminded me of a casting-off I had just invented when I last saw her, and which I was all

18. TIGHT CASTING-OFF

24

steamed up about. In the meantime I had completely forgotten about it, so have just had to re-invent it. It is very
decorative, extremely tight and firm, and goes as follows:

Knit 3 stitches. Pull the first over the other two. Knit a
fourth stitch. Pull the second stitch over the third and fourth.
Knit a fifth stitch. Pull the third stitch over the fourth and
fifth. And so on; like regular casting-off, except with three
stitches instead of two. If you work it with an extremely
large needle, it can be made comparatively loose.

Casting-off at shoulders

5. Can anything be done about those steps that appear
when you are casting off the shoulder-back at the rate of, for
instance, five stitches at the beginning of each row? Yes,
indeed. Here is a neat trick which I learned from a master-
knitter many years ago. Instead of casting off, for instance,
five stitches at the beginning of the rows, get rid of one of
the stitches at the end of the previous row, by working the

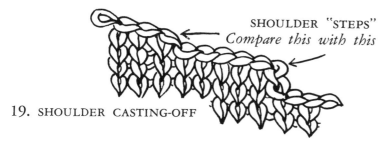

SHOULDER "STEPS"
Compare this with this

19. SHOULDER CASTING-OFF

last two stitches together; then you only have to cast off four
stitches. This is sheer magic, and your shoulder line will
have only an almost imperceptible wave, instead of a wicked
step. Thank you, Mrs. Neumann.

Decreasing

1. I'm sure you know one way of decreasing—just work
two stitches together (K2 tog.)—but some knitters are not
too familiar with its fraternal twin, slip one, knit one, pass

20. KNIT 2 TOGETHER

21. SL1, K1, PSSO
OR SKP

22. SSK

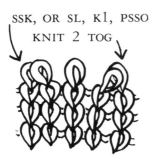

SSK, OR SL, K1, PSSO

KNIT 2 TOG

23. DECREASING

slipped stitch over, or sl 1, K1, psso, for short, or, even shorter, SKP.

2. Barbara Walker has, in masterly fashion, transmuted sl 1, K1, psso into SSK (slip, slip, knit), which presents an infinitely neater appearance, as well as being easier to execute, once you get the hang of it. It is also quicker to write and easier on the tongue and teeth; try it. I quote her: "SSK: slip the first and second stitches *knitwise,* one at a time, then insert the tip of left-hand needle into the *fronts* of these two stitches from the left, and knit them together from this position."

When decreases come in pairs, as they frequently do, you should always employ both of these methods, or your shaping will not appear symmetrical. Which one you use first and which second is up to you, depending on the final results wanted, but be consistent. Knit two together (K2 tog) leans to the right, and slip, slip, knit (SSK) leans to the left, according to whether it is the stitch to the right or to the left which is being eliminated by the decrease. You will soon develop a preference in using these methods, and then a habit.

Some knitters have trouble keeping their paired decreases in a strict vertical line; I would advise them to mark the stitches (one, two, or three) between the decreases, and to see to it that these stitches remain inviolate, and never involved in the decreasing.

3. If you wish to decrease two stitches in one fell swoop, then slip one, knit two together, and pass the slipped stitch over. A neat variant of this is to slip two stitches at once, knit one, and pass both slipped stitches over it.

Increasing

1. There are many ways to increase, but I find myself almost invariably using one which is not too widely recog-

26

nized, namely, Make one (M1). This is quite simply achieved by putting a firm backward loop over the right needle (A). The result is the same as that accomplished by picking up the running thread between the stitches and knitting into the back of it (twisting it), which produces the effect of the stitch having been made a row sooner. I think my way is faster, and anyway I like it, and I'm used to it. It is the best increase for pairing that I know, as it is a totally separate stitch, made independently of any other and standing all by itself between its neighbors. If you are a perfectionist, you may make the loop as above for the first increase of a pair, and then reverse it for the second (B)— then your shaping will be absolutely symmetrical. But this is, as I said, sheer perfectionism. Try it out and see if you think it is worth it.

24.

25. MAKE ONE (M.I.) INCREASE BY BACKWARD LOOP

2. The most invisible increase of all is here illustrated. It is formed by knitting into the stitch of the row below from the back; *not* from the front. That is to say, twist it. I think you will notice quite a difference.

26. PRACTICALLY INVISIBLE INCREASE

Sewing-up

This is second only to purling as a knitters' nemesis, which is why I avoid it where possible in designing. Experts can backstitch a seam from the wrong side, and have it come out creditably (if somewhat bulkily), but it is very difficult for the average knitter, who is possibly not fond of sewing.

If you have landed yourself with five pieces of sweater to be sewn together, try tackling the job from the right side, where you can at least see what you are doing, and how it's going to look. Start with the shoulder seams, which are nearly always cast off. I rarely weave them, as a sweater needs all the firmness it can muster at this point, and weaving stretches too much. Since it is inadvisable to make the seams invisible, why not make them decorative? To this end, cast off in purl, or even work one row of purl before casting off. Then the seam may be sewn over and over, firmly, stitch for stitch. You may take one stitch from each side alternately, if you wish, so long as the seam lies flat, and is firm.

Side seams for stocking stitch may successfully be "woven" vertically, as described in any knitting magazine. This forms a seam which is almost invisible until it is stretched sideways. But why not make side seams decorative too? Keep two or three stitches at each end in garter stitch, by beginning and ending the purl rows with K2, or K3. Slip all first stitches unless you belong to the school which frowns—or even scowls—on this practice. An edge of this kind is good-looking, and doesn't curl much, and it may be most successfully joined by taking a knot from each side alternately. Garter stitch garments are sewn up this way, and have almost invisible seams. The ridges of garter stitch also make the rows easier to count, and ensure your having the same number of rows on front and on back.

Don't be distressed if your sewing-up fails to please you; you are in the same boat with many excellent knitters. Do as I did; abolish sewing-up altogether by making seamless sweaters. There are several examples later in this book, and I think you will enjoy them.

28

Weaving, or Grafting, or Kitchener Stitch

Although this is considered a rare and esoteric skill, it is surprisingly simple if you keep your head. Watch the route of your weaving-wool sharply as you progress, and keep it in the correct path. Don't worry about looseness; tension is adjusted at the end.

1. *Stocking stitch weaving.* See to it that your fabric is evenly divided on two needles, wrong sides together. Break the wool, leaving a good working length, and thread it through a large blunt wool needle. Name the needles "Front Needle" (nearest to you), and "Back Needle" (farthest from you). Now:

*Pull wool through 1st st on Front Needle as if to knit. Take stitch off. Pull wool through 2nd st on Front Needle as if to purl. Leave stitch on. Pull wool through 1st st on Back Needle as if to purl. Take stitch off. Pull wool through 2nd st on Back Needle as if to knit. Leave stitch on. Repeat from *, and keep repeating. You will soon see that it is perfectly practicable to perform both movements on each needle in one fell swoop. When weaving is finished, adjust tension of weaving-wool. If you notice some purled stitches, it is because you have put the blunt needle the wrong way through the stitch, and this is worth undoing, and doing over again.

2. *Garter stitch weaving* is even simpler, but you must be careful to have the correct sides of the fabric together, or you may end up having two "purled" rows too close together or too far apart. The best way to ensure that the fabric is facing the right way is to have the working threads hanging together at the right end when starting to weave. Break off one, and weave with the other. When finishing a pointed garter stitch hood, knit to the middle of the row and fold the sides together.

Now keep working the first two steps of stocking stitch weaving: *Pull wool through first st on Front Needle as if to knit. Take stitch off. Pull wool through second st on Front Needle as if to purl. Leave stitch on. Repeat from * on Back Needle, and keep repeating on both needles alternately. Adjust tension.

Ribbing, or any patterned fabric, may be woven *if* the grain of the pieces is running the same way. That is to say, you can weave the top of one piece to the bottom of another piece, but you *cannot* weave the tops of two pieces together; the pattern will be half a stitch off. Two tops can only be woven together in stocking stitch or in garter stitch. There is no sense in weaving unless the result is absolutely undetectable; if this is impossible I think it is better to have a good honest organic seam.

Borders

My current favorite is the *garter stitch border,* which is easy, firm, flat, and the same on both sides. When pulled laterally, it loses its rather "kindergarten" appearance, and looks mysterious, like an Unknown Stitch. I have devised a buttonhole which almost disappears into it. Why don't you try just one garter stitch border and see how it suits your taste and temperament?

Suppose you have a nice cardigan on hand, finished except for the front and neck borders. Take a pair of 14″ needles one or two sizes smaller than those used for the body of the sweater; a long circular needle will do too. Starting at the lower right-hand corner, with the right side of your work towards you, knit up one stitch in each of the first two rows of your knitting. Do this about one and a half or two stitches in from the front edge, wherever the knitted fabric starts to look tidy and even. Skip the third row, and knit up a stitch in each of the fourth and fifth rows. Skip the sixth row; work into the seventh and eighth rows, and so on up the front. You will have two-thirds as many knitted-up stitches as there are rows, which will give a border that neither puckers, flares, nor droops. When you come to the neck, knit up around it, stitch for stitch, and so on down the other side. You will notice that I say "knit up" and not "pick up." This means that you are better off pulling the wool through with the needle for each stitch. Some people pick up the stitches with the needle, and then knit them off. I think that this is because the term "pick up" has misled them.

Now work the border, back and forth, in all-knit, increasing two stitches every second row at center neck front, for a mitered corner. For a reverse-miter—if I may so express myself—at inner corners, decrease two stitches every second row. You may keep the actual corner stitch in stocking stitch on the right side, by purling it on the wrong side, and then, of course the mitering increases or decreases are worked on either side of the corner stitch.

Buttonholes (see p. 39), if any, should be placed at half the desired border width—after perhaps three or four ridges. On the row on which they are made you may wish to decrease away about one quarter of the back-of-neck stitches (K2, K2 tog across). This is because of the marked tendency of neck-backs to become loose in their ways. When you have worked about as much again, and the border looks right, cast off, in purl, on the right side.

Borders may also be worked in *seed stitch* of K1, P1, alternated every row.

A border on a garter stitch garment needs a different proportion of stitches to rows—one stitch for every ridge (2 rows). (See p. 90.)

If you have decided on an elastic *ribbed lower edge* for

31

your sweater, do the job thoroughly—put in at least thirty rows of K2, P2, rib. If you want an inelastic border of K1, P1, rib, make it any length you want, from 2″ on up. You may coordinate the front borders by making them also in ribbing. Try to center the ribs at neck-front corners, as this is one of the spots on a sweater where stitch-perfect knitting pays off.

These words are being written on a desert island in the middle of an unpopulated lake in Ontario. It is a sparkling clear day in early September, and I am working on a small experimental sweater-from-the-neck-down. This is not my favorite kind of sweater, and I doubt if it ever will be, since all the excitement and interest of the shoulder shaping comes at the beginning, and one is left with the endless and boring straight body and sleeves to complete. Its one excuse for existing is its indispensability for children, whose sweaters must eternally be repaired and lengthened at the lower edges.

Well; I have finished the sleeves, ending them with ribbing at the wrists, and am approaching the lower end of the body on a hundred stitches. I am faced with still more ribbing, and a cast-off edge, which is hard to do neatly and elastically in ribbing. I am discouraged. Let us see if ruse and subterfuge will solve my problems.

I am greatly helped in my undertaking by having run out of wool. I have been using the classic unsurpassable pale gray Shetland—six stitches to one inch. The only other wool I have is some handsome cocoa-colored 2-ply Sheepwool—five stitches to one inch.

Now all wools have their optimum GAUGE for specific purposes and *knitting* worked at *six* stitches to one inch in *wool* which is best suited to *five* stitches to one inch would have a hard, thick, unyielding texture, fine for a wind- and waterproof sweater for a large mariner, but no use to a small child. I must somehow combine it with Shetland and come up with an acceptable result.

Whichever way you slice it, the sweater will have a heavy border, as the new wool is so much thicker. Let us turn the unavoidable to good advantage, and finish with an honest heavy border of garter stitch. First I will blend the two colors and textures by the use of a small-repeat one-to-one pattern. After two inches of this I will put in one purl round, then three rounds of knit, having abandoned the gray Shetland at the end of the pattern. The work will start to flare out, as a hundred stitches in Shetland measure 16½″, while in Sheepswool at five stitches to one inch they measure 20″. So in the last of the three rounds I will decease 25% to 75 stitches by working K2, K2 together, around; firstly because of the thicker wool; secondly because garter stitch has a lateral spread; thirdly because the bottom of any sweater needs holding in. All right; then one purl round, then two

☐ GREY

✕ BROWN

— GREY (PURL)

✳ BROWN (PURL)

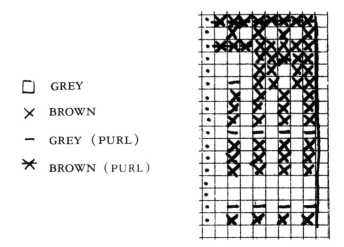

BORDER-PATTERN IN TWO WEIGHTS OF WOOL FOR CHILD'S SWEATER. (START AT BOTTOM; WORK FROM R TO L. REP FROM DOT.)

rounds of knit, then one round of purl; knit one round; purl one round, and finish off by casting off in purl. Just a minute while I do it.

It worked. And would have worked just as well in all Shetland, but without such a sharp decrease. The purled cast-off neatly conceals its extreme looseness. For an adult sweater I would, of course, make the whole border longer, and work five or six knit rounds between the first two purl rounds before tapering down to nothing. I think it would look just as good. I'll not venture to say that a border like this has never been made before—there is nothing new under the changing moon—but I *will* say I've never seen one.

Necessity is the mother of invention.

It saddens me to think of all the things I may "invent" too late to be included in this book.

Another good way to make a lower border is with a *hem*. Knitted hems have found much favor during the last ten years or so, but I have yet to see one that is logically designed. Most of them show a lamentable inclination to flare out, right? Very occasionally, directions will admonish you to work hems tightly on smaller needles. But why do no printed directions suggest having less stitches for the inside of the hem than for the body of the sweater? Just 10% less will do it, or fewer, if you wish. For a 200-stitch sweater, cast on 180 stitches, work an inch or so for the hem, then K9, Make 1, around. Knit one more round, purl one round for a sharp turn, and sail away on and up your sweater.

My favorite way is the reverse of this; start the sweater with *no* hem at the lower edge—just regular casting-on—and during the days and weeks of knitting, meditate on this hem. Shall it be a different color? A bright one or a subtle? Shall it contain a modest pattern? You'll have plenty of time to make up your mind.

34

When the time comes to start the hem you may either knit up one stitch in every cast-on stitch, and purl one round, or knit up in the loops just behind the cordlike round of casting-on. This gives an unusually neat turn, and a purl

27. KNITTING-UP FROM CAST-ON EDGE

round is unnecessary. In either case knit one round before you decrease, and then K8, K2 together around for a 10% decrease. You may have your decreases even closer together if you want a snugger hem. Use your judgment. You may include any small pattern that appeals to you, in a different color, or the name of the recipient of your labors, or any motto, axiom, or family joke that seems appropriate. The

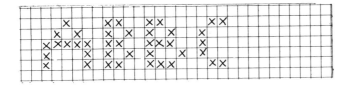

letters of the alphabet are quite easily worked out on squared paper, and need take no more than five stitches in height. Few names can fill the entire circumference of a sweater, so join the pattern-wool anew every time you come to the first letter; this means only five threads to darn in on either side. You may care to fill the space with stars or flowers. Be careful not to knit LEON XUEYOJ—it has been known to happen. You'll have to decide for yourself which way up the legend should be—towards the wearer or towards admiring friends —I've not yet made up my mind about it.

When the hem is the length you want it—anything from 1½″ on—do not cast off. I rarely cast off if I can avoid it, and beginning and intermediate knitters may also welcome a way of avoiding it. Anyway, hems are much better off without a tight, neat or, alternatively, a loose, untidy casting-off. Break your wool at a respectable length, and thread it through a very large, very sharp wool needle. Take out the knitting needle; without screaming, please; the stitches can't go anywhere; and—for the first few times, anyway—baste the hem flat with thread. Few things look worse than a hem pulled up so tightly that the sewing-stitches make dimples on the right side, or so loosely that the hem itself shows below the fold line. Sew the hem down, stitch for stitch, taking just a skimming of the sweater fabric, and keeping the stitches good and loose, so that the hem will stretch as much as the sweater if necessary.

And there you are. Give it a breathy patting on the wrong side with the steam iron, and you will find that you have a fine, flat, unflaring hem. If worked in finer wool than the sweater proper, it will lie even flatter. In finer wool I also decrease 10%. Or nearly always.

A very pretty way of turning a hem is to work Yarn over, K2 together for one round. The resulting row of holes has a fine natural turn. It looks best on women's and children's clothes.

Phoney Seams

Opponents of circular sweaters—and there are unfortunately some—take as one argument the theory that being without seams, circular sweaters don't hang together properly. A fallacious argument if ever I heard one, but let us refute it by putting in imitation seams, which are rather good things anyway, and a neat and mysterious feat of skill to boot. They may be made by slipping the seam

36

stitch every second round, but this is a rather tiresome thing to remember while you are peacefully working your way up your lovely circular sweater, with no interruptions, and thinking great thoughts. Phoney seams are great fun to make later, and the technique will, I think, prove to you that you are the absolute boss of your knitting.

Before you cast off, find the exact side or seam stitch, and drop it clear down to the first round of body or sleeve underarm. This makes, of course, a monstrous runner. Take a crochet hook, put it through the stitch of the first round, and hook the next two stitches through it together. Then one stitch, then two together again, then one stitch, then two, and so on, up to the top of the piece.

28. PHONEY SEAM

You will have ⅔ as many rows in the "seam" as in the garment itself. This forms a very efficient-looking vertical ridge which almost appears pressed in, and is absolutely ineradicable. It not only looks well, but it also helps greatly when the time comes for blocking or for folding the sweater.

You can even make a phoney seam on a old, already-completed sweater. Snip one stitch at the underarm, and let a stitch down from there in both directions, later repairing the original snip by weaving—it will never show. In the case of sleeves, be careful that the runner doesn't become involved in the shaping at the lower sleeve underarm. If this happens, stop the runner right there. It is to guard against this contingency that I leave three full stitches between sleeve decreases or increases.

Pockets

I have only one pocket which is not available in any of the good knitting books. I call it the Afterthought Pocket, as you really don't have to give it a thought until the garment is finished. Try on your new, nicely blocked sweater, look in the glass, and make a wish for pockets; your wish is as good as granted. Decide where you wish you had thought to put them; I like them at the point where my middle finger hits my hip bone. Mark the exact point, and horrors! snip one thread of one stitch right there. Measure exactly, and make an identical snip on the other side. You will think you now have the genesis of two appalling holes, but you are deceived. Unravel the cut ends carefully for ten stitches to right and to left, and you will have made a neat 20-stitch opening. This opening will be edged with 40 little stitches, pleading to be picked up. Pick them up; two sock needles for the top ones and one sock needle for the bottom ones. Take wool and the fourth needle, and start knitting around, from the right side. If you remember to purl the bottom 20 stitches on the first round, your front pocket-edge will have a good sharp fold-line. When you have worked far enough to have achieved a pocket of the depth you want, weave (or even sew) front and back together, and pop the pocket into place. Neaten the two corners with the un-ravelled wool. Now aren't you proud of yourself? Go ahead and put pockets everywhere you've always wanted them. If you can't match the wool, pretend you wanted them in a contrasting color. I have been known to take out a pair of pockets in an ancient sweater which had sagged unaccount-ably (yes, Virginia, this can happen to anybody), and put them in again higher up. The original pockets had been snipped and unravelled, so the scar was totally invisible. There *is* a similar pocket for which you plan ahead by knitting in a thread of contrasting wool, but this one cannot be caused to disappear without a trace. Besides, what's the sense of planning ahead unless you have to? You spend so many hours knitting, your thoughts running in and out with your needles; how satisfying not to be committed to too many details in advance, and to be able to incorporate later some of the new ideas that come to you while you are doing the donkey-work.

Buttonholes

There has been a regular boiling-up of these recently, so that there is no longer any excuse for making pigseyes. You are surely familiar with one of the several versions of the one-row buttonhole.

Here is my own three-row button-hole, which I still use almost always: Row 1. Cast off the required number of

29. 3-ROW BUTTONHOLE

stitches, very often three. Row 2. Cast on the same number of stitches by the primitive method of making three backward loops over the right needle. Pick up the first stitch you cast off in the previous row (it should have the same running-thread as the stitch next to it; the first one on the left needle). Put this stitch on the left needle and knit two together. Row 3. Quite simple. When you come to the three cast-on stitches, knit into the back of each, and also into the back of the stitch immediately following them. Buttonhole completed.

The two stitch-tightening techniques used here—picking up an odd stitch and knitting it together with its neighbor, and twisting a stitch by knitting into the back of it—will prove true friends on many occasions. The first helps when a hole is made by turning in the middle of a row and working back (pick up a thread where it looks loosest—experiment—and knit it together with the stitch proper). The

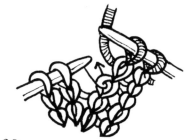

30. TURNING FOR SHORT ROW

39

second helps when that tricky hole appears at the ankles of socks (knit into the back of the loose stitch). It is little dodges like these that make a craft a joy; some of them one picks up from friends and enemies; some of them one discovers for oneself.

2. Here is another buttonhole. This is its first appearance on any stage—it's only a year old, the little thing, and is chiefly aimed at experienced and courageous knitters. That ought to put you on your mettle. It is useful primarily in two-needle sweaters where the border is incorporated with the body of the garment, and where you are not quite sure where you want the buttonholes to be. Hark back to the Afterthought Pocket (p. 37) and snip just one thread at the center of where the buttonhole is to be: Unravel only slightly—three stitches on the bottom and three on the top are usually enough. Now hark back again, this time to Sewn Casting-off (p. 23) and cast off the stitches by this method. When you come to the last stitch on the bottom, treat the stitch next to it (the one in the fabric) the same way, and then continue across the top. Fasten the end and the be-

31. AFTERTHOUGHT BUTTONHOLE

ginning securely, and finish off the short ravelled ends by resourcefully darning your needle in and out before you thread it. This buttonhole is not nearly as tricky as it sounds, but for goodness' sake make a few practice ones before you put the first one in an actual sweater. You may like to use finer matching wool. If this is not available, split your wool, and twist it tighter before working with it. If you have mastered "casting-on casting-off" (p. 33), here is a good opportunity to try it.

The enormous advantage of this buttonhole is that it can be added when a garment is completed, and you know exactly where you want the buttons to be. It is not always too easy to determine this when you put in the buttonholes on the way up. Sometimes you end up with the top one and its neighbor being too close for comfort, or disturbingly far apart. Of course, one way out of the dilemma is to make the button side first. Hold it up against you and space the buttons as you want them. Then all you have to do is make matching buttonholes on the other side.

The Best Way I Know to Split Wool

Unwind a yard or so from the ball, and anchor it with a needle. Climb up on a chair, take some of the plies in one hand and some in the other, and pull gently. The ball will spin giddily, and the wool will unwind. Keep repeating this process, which is faster and more effective than you would think. If you inhabit a stately mansion with an imposing staircase, you can do many yards at a time. The top of a tall building would be better still, but you would be at the mercy of the winds and practical jokers.

Small Headaches Discovered Several Rows Down

Twisted stitches, dropped stitches, split yarn stitches, or inadvertently "made" stitches may be neatly remedied by your trusty crochet hook. Trace the offending stitch up to the needle, work to this point, and then let the stitch run down to where the trouble is. Actually, the word "run" is inaccurate, as, contrary to superstition, a dropped stitch does not immediately zoom down to the bottom of your work like a run in a stocking. At the most it will slither down one or two rows, and cling there, moaning piteously, and waiting to be picked up; if it has to descend any

41

further, it must be helped. When you get it to where the trouble is, fix the error, and crochet-hook the stitch up again. Your intelligence will tell you when to hook it to the front and when to the back, if you are using a pattern containing both knit and purl stitches. If you don't get it right the first time, let it down again, and give it another try. It can, and should, be perfect. In the case of a dropped stitch from several rows back, the job will be a tight one; it has been ignored for several rows, and there is not sufficient wool in the succeeding rows with which to hook it up. You therefore have to borrow wool from the stitches each side of it every row.

If you are eliminating an unnecessarily "made" stitch, the reverse is true, and the slack must be pulled sideways to be absorbed by the stitches to right and left. Try to look at your work objectively every few rows, to check when things like this have occurred, so that you can catch them before they become too deeply entrenched.

I once discovered a contrary cable right at the beginning of an almost finished sweater. I let down a giant runner of six stitches to where the error was, picked up the six on a short sock needle, corrected the cable, and knitted my way up again, with six stitches and two short needles, from right to left, and working the cables as they came. It looked a bit cockeyed until it was blocked, and yanked into seemliness while damp and steamy, but then it was completely unnoticeable.

I wouldn't take this trouble any more, by the way, but would snip one stitch a couple of rows above the error, let down the stitches, correct the error, knit the stitches up again, and then weave the snipped row back in. I am truly boss of my knitting. I would also eliminate an indelible stain this way, if it wasn't too big, by extracting and replacing the offending rows, one at a time.

42

Joining Wool

Mrs. Zimmermann, how do you join in a new ball of yarn? Do you always join at a seam? My dear, my sweaters usually have no seams, and besides, as a knitter with reverence for her material, I hate to waste an inch of wool.

Do you split the yarn and twist half the plies of one piece with half the plies of another? No; too lazy. And this is troublesome to do perfectly anyway.

Do you tie in your yarn? Heavens, a KNOT? Let me put an end to this catechism and tell you that I join in a new ball of wool, always, by working just one stitch with both wools together, the old and the new, leaving 3″ tails hanging down on the wrong side. These are later darned in lightly for about an inch, with a large sharp needle, and snipped off. And I defy you to tell from the right side where this was accomplished. A perfectionist may take out one of the ends from this double stitch, make half a square knot with both ends, and darn in lightly as above, after checking the tension carefully on the right side.

When joining in a different colored wool, the above method is of course impractical, as a double stitch with two colors would be unsightly. I just start knitting with the new color, leaving two tails and a looseness. When the work is finished I must admit to making a square knot (after adjusting the tension very carefully) before darning the ends in. Why I do this with different colors and not with wools of the same color, I can't tell you—superstition perhaps. But one thing is certain—never knit a knot. No matter how careful you are to keep it on the wrong side, it usually pops through to the right side to haunt you. There is a strong human inclination to regard knots in new wool as acts of God, and to knit on. Don't. Break the wool at the knot and treat it like a regular join. If the skein has an unusual number of knots—say more than three—drop a card to the manufacturer, telling him the dye lot. If he is on his toes, he will be grateful.

Now comes what I perhaps inflatedly call my philosophy of knitting. Like many philosophies, it is hard to express in a few words. Its main tenets are enjoyment and satisfaction, accompanied by thrift, inventiveness, an appearance of industry, and, above all, resourcefulness.

Resourcefulness is probably the key word.

Primitive societies herded sheep, presumably for milk, meat, and skins. How resourceful to gather stray tufts of wool from thorns and briars and spin them into yarn. How resourceful to experiment with knots and loops on two sticks, and eventually to resolve the tangle into the prototype of some form of knitted fabric. Weaving took place at home, but knitting could accompany the shepherd, the sailor, the woman walking to the fields, anybody who at any time had idle hands.

Today knitting can still fill odd moments. Think of the frustrating periods of time we spend just waiting; waiting for the coffee to boil; waiting in the car; waiting until the fish bite; waiting until somebody else's favorite program is over and we can switch channels; we all have our own particular waits. Those who ride daily to work could finish a sock in a week if they would spend the time knitting. Imagine! Twenty-five pairs of socks a year. Twenty-five Christmas present problems solved. Have you realized how most men yearn for proper socks? Men I hardly know at all are constantly and wistfully and broadly hinting that I make them a pair. Sometimes I do. My own husband is so well supplied that I practically never have to mend any socks, as the wear is spread out over so many pairs. It's like the women who get married with a dozen dozen sheets and towels; you never see *them* at the white sales.

So there is knitting as a time filler. As a brace for the

human spirit it is just as effective. How gratifying it is to see one's family warmly, comfortably, and even fashionably dressed in garments that really suit and fit them, and which will fit their siblings in time to come. Don't say to the younger child, "Here is Sebastian's old sweater that you may as well wear out." Say, instead, "Sebastian is growing so fast that he can't wear his favorite beautiful sweater any more. Let's wash it, and mend it, and put it in a plastic bag, and when you are big enough, perhaps he will let you wear it." Resourceful? You bet. When making a cardigan I always put buttonholes on both sides, so that it can change its gender easily. Girls love to wear boys' sweaters, but, strangely, the reverse is far from true.

I try to convince myself that I have no favorite sweaters, although I always make a great fuss over the latest designed, but I am especially fond of those constructed on the resourceful elimination of two of the most common knitters' dislikes —the dislike of purling and the dislike of sewing-up. The second is an expensive dislike, as it is so strong that one will pay to have the sewing-up done by somebody else. Let nobody say she can't sew up a sweater—she just doesn't want to. Reminds me of the infuriating remark, "I've always wanted to knit, but I just can't." Pish, my good woman, you can plan meals, can't you? You can put your hair up? You can type, write fairly legibly, shuffle cards? All of these are more difficult than knitting. You just don't want to knit, so why pretend that you do? It's not compulsory; take up something else.

Seamless circular sweaters solve both the problem of purling and of sewing-up, and are actually very logical besides.

The human being is so constructed that it can be completely covered by a series of shaped tubes. Tailors and dressmakers succeed excellently and skillfully in making tubes out of flat woven material; their achievements are nothing short of marvelous. But we, the humble knitters, can fabricate natural-born tubes by the very nature of our craft of circular knitting. With the techniques of increasing and decreasing at our command, we can shape or even bend the tubes as we will, without seams, gussets, or darts. It is then only a matter of uniting the various tubes by knitting them together, or sometimes weaving them together, and we could, if he desired them, make long-johns for an octopus.

Later chapters in this book contain examples of my seam-less sweaters more or less in the order in which they were designed. The first is a ski sweater with classic dropped shoulders, which is not entirely seamless, as the armholes are cut. Then come the true seamless ones, yoke sweater, raglan, saddle-shoulder, and the new "Hybrid." As far as I can see, that just about wraps up the possibilities, but I have been fooled before in like circumstances, and who can tell?

Thus you will see that out of my innocent aversion to purling and sewing-up have come comfortable and func-tional sweaters, which hundreds—perhaps thousands—of knitters enjoy so much that they make them again and again.

All designs given are for 40″ sweaters on 200 stitches at a gauge of 5 stitches to 1″. They may be varied endlessly by changing the color, the gauge and the stitch. The percentages I give for measurements are meant for the average person, and which of us is truly average? After you have made one of these sweaters, you may wish to change the percent-ages a bit to suit your taste, or the shape of the wearer. Feel free. I shall have failed in my endeavor if you copy my designs too slavishly; they are intended only as a guide, so be your own designer. No two people knit alike, look alike, think alike; why should their projects be alike? Your sweater should be like your own favorite original recipes—like nobody else's on earth.

And a good thing too.

Chapter 2

Gauge: Required Reading

IF you are an inexperienced, or perhaps unsuccessful, knitter, you *must* read this chapter (a short, pithy one), or all is lost.

GAUGE is the most important principle in knitting.

It means the number of stitches, and fractions of a stitch, that YOU YOU YOU achieve to 1″ with the wool and needles you plan to use.

Any wool has an optimum GAUGE for a given purpose, and this GAUGE is given at the beginning of all printed directions. It is vitally important to achieve it; keep changing needle sizes until you do.

At the risk of disagreeing with the Establishment, may I stress that you be prepared to disregard any needle SIZE recommended in knitting books? It must be considered only as an approximate suggestion.

People knit so differently in matters of tightness or looseness that it is totally impossible to recommend one size of needle for everybody. Most unfortunately, the size recommended is frequently very large in proportion, so that a trusting beginner is obliged to work inordinately tightly in order to achieve the desired GAUGE.

47

For instance, a size 8 needle is often recommended for a GAUGE of 5 stitches to one inch in knitting worsted. Now I am only a moderately loose knitter, but I can quite easily achieve the same GAUGE with a needle three sizes smaller— a size 5. I see no reason to make myself nervous by knitting very tightly on a size 8 just because the book says so. I enjoy knitting loosely, and thus can attain the same GAUGE with a smaller needle, and I advise you to try the same thing.

You *must* make a swatch before casting on a project to see what your own GAUGE is. I know this is a hateful job, so why not make a larger swatch, and call it a cap? Then it will be useful, and possibly become quite popular. You don't have to finish it before you begin your sweater; a few inches will suffice for measurement.

For circular knitting a cap is even preferable to a swatch. Some of us knit more tightly than we purl, or contrariwise, and a circular cap is made round and round in all knit, just as a circular sweater will be.

Very well, then if directions specify a GAUGE of 5 sts to 1″, cast on about 90 stitches on a 16″ circular needle, and work around in the pattern stitch for 3″- 4″. Take out the needle and lay your work flat. With a ruler measure off 3″ in the center of the knitted fabric, and place two pins exactly 3″ apart. Carefully count the number of stitches between the pins. One stitch looks like this, ⑴ two stitches look like this, ⑴⑴ and so on. Do not neglect to count half stitches and even one-third stitches, if there are any.

Divide the number of stitches and fractions of a stitch in 3″ by 3. The result may be:

15, which, divided by three, gives a GAUGE of 5 sts to 1″.
16, which, divided by three, gives a GAUGE of 5⅓ sts to 1″.
14, which, divided by three, gives a GAUGE of 4⅔ sts to 1″.

Now; if you are following directions which call for a GAUGE of 5 sts to 1″, you *must* achieve this GAUGE exactly, or the sweater will come out the wrong size. If you are even ¼ stitch off GAUGE on a 200-stitch, 40″ sweater, it will end up over 2″ too big or—far worse—too small.

So 15 sts to 3″ is perfect; 16 sts to 3″ is too tight; 14 sts to 3″ is too loose.

Keep changing needle sizes until you are working at a GAUGE of exactly 15 sts to 3″, which is 5 sts to 1″.

If you are working on a design of your own, you may be much more independent. It is quite possible that you prefer a tighter or a looser GAUGE. Then all you have to do is to establish this GAUGE, multiply it by the number of inches around your sweater-to-be, and the result is the number of stitches to cast on.

It's that simple.

But extremely important.

End of Chapter 2.

(P.S. Better not finish that cap until the sweater is done; you may conceivably need the wool out of which it is made.)

(P.P.S. Some directions give you the vertical row gauge as well as the horizontal stitch gauge. I have yet to find a good use for a vertical row gauge, since vertical measurements are much easier to handle in inches.)

49

Chapter 3

Ski Sweater in Color Patterns

It all started when the children wanted ski sweaters, back in the palmy days when ski sweaters were a rarity, and sometimes a funny-looking rarity at that. They often had rampant Christmas trees or deer prancing at each other across the chest. Back, front, and sleeves were made separately, entailing the purling of every second row, and thus the working of color patterns on the wrong side every second row, with the yarn carried in front. Armholes were shaped; sleeves had caps to them and were sometimes laboriously designed to match the chest patterns. Shoulders frequently sagged.

Against such pitiful objects I resolutely set my face.

Now we had in the family a vintage and genuine Norwegian sweater. Every time I had occasion to mend the front bands, I noticed an inordinate number of wool ends, and it finally dawned on me that the thing had been made round and round, possibly on circular needles, and CUT down the front. On examining an armhole seam, I found that this had been cut too. It became obvious that the knitter of *this* sweater had not been obliged to work back and forth in color patterns.

Encouraged by this discovery, and by the conviction that what a Norwegian can do, a Limey can copy, I cast on a likely number of stitches in rather pretty silver-gray heather knitting worsted, and conscientiously ribbed thirty rounds on a circular needle. For the color pattern I took some white wool, which I happened to have lying around. Need I say that I didn't have enough of it lying around, and that this was when I found out that white, too, has dye lots? I started out with the classic "Ljus"—one white stitch in four every fourth round—and somehow had the wit to keep the carried wool very loose on the inside.

Before long the two wools were in a terrible tangle, because I kept picking up the "new" wool from under the "old" one, as all knitting directions admonish one to do. Thinking to myself that a Norwegian would have given up knitting after the first mitten under such conditions, I tried *not* twisting the wools, but taking them from over and under each other alternately. This worked.

All knitting books may now sue me, but I am convinced that the injunction to twist yarns is totally redundant.

It is possibly a relic of the great Argyll Era, when the pattern wool was wound on bobbins. It was not carried along the back of the work, but twisted round the Main Color when no longer needed, and left hanging there until needed again. In a case like this it is absolutely necessary to twist the yarns. You are making several little pieces of different-colored knitting, linked to each other at their edges. If you don't link them by twisting the wools they would remain what they are—little pieces of different-colored knitting.

But Norwegian color pattern knitting and the making of Scottish Argylls have a watery waste between them as deep and wide as the North Sea or German Ocean. They are completely different techniques, and should not be confused.

51

If you want to pick up the new color from under the old one, feel free. But it is not necessary; I will stick out my neck and say not even desirable.

The above revelation heartened me considerably. It proved to me that The Books don't know everything. They know a great deal, but not everything. Take anything you find in an instruction book, including this one, with a large grain of salt. If it doesn't make sense in your particular circumstances, pay no attention to it; seek further. There are scores of different ways of doing things in knitting, and none of them are wrong, but they are sometimes unsuitable.

There is no right way to knit; there is no wrong way to knit.

The way to knit is the way that suits you, and the way that suits the wool and the pattern and the shape that you are currently working on. Show me any "mistake" and I will show you that it is only a misplaced pattern or an inappropriate technique. There are patterns that include dropped stitches and twisted stitches. There are projects which should be as tight as you can possibly knit; there are others where you have to relax to the point of lethargy in order to make them loose enough. I've not yet found a pattern which includes a split stitch; this is the only real mistake I know.

So if anybody kindly tells you that what you are doing is "wrong," don't take umbrage; they mean well. Smile submissively, and listen, keeping your disagreement on an entirely mental level. They may be right, in this particular case, and even if not, they may drop off pieces of information which will come in very handy if you file them away carefully in your brain for future reference.

This digression leaves me still working my way up my first ski sweater, having discovered that the wools didn't tangle if I compensated for every twist by twisting the other way alternately—in fact by not twisting at all.

But I was still dropping the gray wool every time I came to a white stitch in order to pick up the white wool, and then having to change back again. I tried carrying both wools together, and selecting the one I needed. This worked, but it was slow, and it tended to tighten up the knitted fabric—for me, anyway.

Then my childhood came back to me, all in a rush. Why couldn't I carry the white wool in the OTHER HAND? I could, indeed. Of course I was lucky in that I could knit both ways. To those of you familiar with only one way of knitting, the best advice I can give is to learn the other way immediately if you want to knit any color patterns. It will be slow at first, but you will soon speed up, and you will find that it is faster than dropping and picking up the wool for every color change. With practice, it is almost as fast as knitting and purling, and much more interesting, naturally. It is rather wonderful to see the patterns gradually taking shape under one's needles—almost like very skilled drawing.

Further examination of the old sweater revealed that its knitter had allowed herself to carry the wool up to five stitches, but never more. So here again I must disagree with the Books which give the innocent and unsuspecting knitter patterns in which the wool is carried for more than five stitches. If one wants to go to all the trouble of carrying the wool for great distances, and of twisting it behind the work so that no monstrous loops occur, that's fine. But it isn't necessary, and it isn't the way classic Norwegian sweaters are made. In fact, the twisting of wools on the wrong side can sometimes adversely affect the appearance of your knitting. If you knit very tightly, the twists may not show, but they *will* show if you are knitting at the usual GAUGE of five

53

stitches to one inch in knitting worsted. Carried wool which has been twisted on the wrong side has a tendency to show slightly on the right side, and sometimes to make dimples and unevenness in the smooth fabric of your knitting. Very skillful and slightly tight knitters can manage to avoid this, but frequent twisting is an added burden for the average knitter. Loops of up to five-stitch length are perfectly permissible on the inside of a sweater, and after time and several washings they tend to stick to the inside of the knitted fabric all by themselves.

Therefore arrange to use patterns which do not include spaces of more than five stitches. Larger spaces may be interrupted with small flowers or stars, or even single snow-flakes, to the great improvement of the whole design. There is no law about not changing a single stitch in directions.

So I said to myself aha, I'll stick to small designs too—none of those skiers sliding down *my* sweater. I hunted up an ancient small book of Faroe designs—now, alas, lost and gone—and came to the conclusion, in studying their extreme simplicity, that designs were originally put in Scandinavian sweaters not as ornament, but as a way of carrying two wools at once and thus making a double-thick and double-warm garment; in fact these designs were truly functional.

At this point I broke away from all the then current ski sweater instructions, and became aggressively inventive. I was inspired, of course, by any genuine Scandinavian sweater l could run to earth.

The body of my sweater was a straight, ribbing-edged tube, knitted without interruption right up to the shoulders. The sleeves were started at the cuff, and were tapered regularly (two stitches increased at underarm every fourth round). At underarm-length the sleeves were cast off straight; sleeve-caps were unnecessary, as the straight-cut armholes came right down over the shoulders. Across the

54

chest and upper sleeves I let loose with a motley collection of found and invented small patterns, and by working the final rounds of body and sleeves in a fetching chocolate brown, I accented the flattering, comfortable, and elegant dropped-shoulder line. The result was an understated, original, and somehow lovely sweater.

The companion sweater was made in oatmeal-colored heather wool, also with white patterns and dark-brown trim, and two brown-eyed little girls were kept warm and content through several winters.

This was the first sweater design I ever sold, and thus it occurred to me that I, too. . . .

To those voicing the objection that a sweater, once cut, can never be ravelled and re-knitted, I answer that ravelling and re-knitting are much more talked about than done. If you are addicted to this form of thrift, by all means work your sweaters back and forth.

One more thing; there is a great difference between the color pattern knitting of Scandinavia and that of Fair Isle. The former has a one-color pattern on a one-color background, while true Scottish Fair Isle patterns change both the colors of the pattern and those of the background in one single pattern. Quite complicated and fascinating, and utterly rewarding.

HOW TO MAKE A PATTERNED SKI SWEATER

This is the very simplest of all sweaters in regard to shape; you can let yourself go with the designs and colors in a quite untrammeled way.

The proportions of a ski sweater are governed by the body width, so measure your favorite old sweater, and multiply the inches around by your GAUGE to determine the number of stitches to cast on. Don't omit to make a swatch.

The following directions are for a 40″ sweater at a GAUGE of exactly 5 stitches to 1″, on 200 stitches. This is a useful and usual size. If you want a larger or a smaller sweater, add or subtract 5 stitches for every inch more or less that you want. If you have more, or less, stitches than 200, amend the directions by following the percentages given, taking the body stitches as 100%. Don't be frightened; there aren't many percentages, and they are simple ones.

You will need about five 4oz skeins of knitting worsted for the background and about half as much for the patterns. For the accents, a 2oz skein will be enough, or an odd ball, if you have one.

You will need two circular needles, a 16″ one, and a 24″ one, of a size to give *you* a GAUGE of 5 stitches to 1″—

something between size 5 and size 8, depending on how *you* knit.

Cast on 200 stitches on the 24″ needle, and join, being very careful to see that the stitches are not twisted on the needle. If you want ribbing, do it now; if you are going to have a hem, just start knitting. Knit around for two or three rounds.

Now begin putting in any patterns you like, using those given here, or any others that please you. I have two tentative rules for you:

1. Be careful to use patterns that call for not more than five consecutive horizontal stitches of one color.
2. Avoid like the plague carrying more than two colors at once.

To depart from these admonishments is possible, but, to my mind, quite hazardous. It will add greatly to the difficulty of the project, especially for a beginner. However imperative it seems to "carry" for a larger number of stitches (and thus to have to twist the wool on the wrong side), or however tempting it is to introduce a third color when I already have one in each hand, I stick to these rules strictly. I find it much more stimulating to give the impression or optical illusion of having broken them, than actually to do so. Of course I am speaking entirely for myself; if you have a valid reason to do otherwise, it's up to you.

Mark the first stitch, and be sure to change your pattern rounds at exactly this point, which you can place at the underarm, so that it will not be disturbing. If you are planning a cardigan, it may be at the center-front, and you must then be very careful to center your larger patterns, so that they will match each other in front, and will be even on both sides of the front borders.

Probably not all patterns will fit precisely into your total number of stitches, but in a sweater of this kind it doesn't matter, especially if the patterns are small ones. Of course, if all the patterns are a multiple of a certain number of stitches (ten is quite common), then your sweater body should be divisible by the same number, and they will fit in perfectly. But otherwise don't worry if there is an occasional discrepancy at the beginning of the rounds.

When working with two colors, practice holding one wool in one hand and one wool in the other, so that you will be knitting the right-handed way and the left-handed way alternately. Persevere with this, as it is not nearly as difficult as it sounds. I'm sure you know somebody who knits the way you don't, and there's no reason why you shouldn't swap methods. After a few days it will be almost automatic, let alone pleasant; it is always wonderful to acquire a new skill anyway. You will knit around, with the right side of your work always in view, and, as you watch your designs develop, you may experience the feeling of being another Leonardo, drawing away with both hands together, one doing the patterns, and the other the background.

Have fun working your way up the body. There will be *no shaping* and *no armholes* to bother about, and you can concentrate on the patterns. But I hope not to the exclusion of *reading* what I have *written,* or you may miss some tricks, and live to rue the day.

The trick at the moment is that of carrying your wool loosely—even sloppily—at the back of your work. The desire to have your knitting "neat" on the wrong side must be resisted. Resisted also must be the belief that the loops will catch on things. They won't. After blocking—let alone a few washings—the loops will want to stick to their own fabric, and they will do so. None of them will be more than five stitches long, anyway. There are knitters who believe

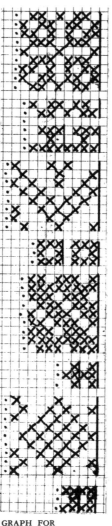

Bottom to middle

GRAPH FOR
SKI-SWEATER.
START AT BOTTOM;
WORK FROM RIGHT
TO LEFT; REPEAT
FROM DOT.
LEAVE ONE, TWO,
OR THREE LINES
BETWEEN PATTERNS.

58

in twisting the wool every third stitch when it is being carried. Let them do it; it concerns nobody but themselves, and is, I believe, a holdover from the period of large widely-spaced patterns on sweaters. I can sincerely enjoin you not to follow this practice; not, at least, until you are a confident and opinionated knitter in your own right. It is much easier my way, and the results are generally conceded to be acceptable.

Hold the color of which there are the most stitches in the hand with which you are most accustomed to knit, and the other color in the other hand. You will have one ball of wool on one side, and one on the other, and never the twain shall twist. Be sure to keep those loops loose. If they end up too loose, (a very remote contingency, indeed), they may be tightened. If they are too tight, you are sunk. Your sweater will be puckery and unpopular.

After the first two or three rounds of a pattern you will find that you hardly have to consult your pattern graph any more, as your eye and brain will tell you where the different-colored stitches fall. Begin with very simple patterns of a two- or three-stitch repeat, and as you gradually work up to more complicated ones of ten- or twelve-stitch repeat I think you will be amazed at how simple it really is.

It is a good idea to make your first ski sweater a "sampler," using a succession of different patterns. This not only makes a very good-looking garment, but it enables you to feel your way with patterns, discovering which ones you prefer, and why. If you use patterns calling for solid blocks of color, the effect will be bold and decisive. A more speckled and airy effect is achieved by using blocks of alternately-colored stitches. Alternate these two types of patterns if you like; experiment.

When the body is the right length for you—somewhere around 27", give or take two or three inches, according to

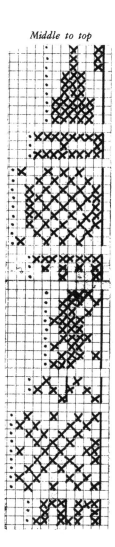

Middle to top

taste, stop knitting, and cast off. If you like, you may cast off the front stitches first, then work back and forth on the back stitches, sloping them (see p. 25) until about ⅓ remain for the neck-back. As stocking stitch likes to curl, I often finish off body- and sleeve-tops with a round or two of purl, sometimes in a different color, and cast off in purl. This not only counteracts the curl, and makes the sewing-in of the sleeves easier, but it also looks well, accentuating, as it does, the elegantly simple dropped-shoulder.

Sleeves are started at the cuff with 20% (one-fifth) of the 200 body stitches, namely 40 stitches, on a 16″ needle. Cast on very loosely, so that 40 stitches will stretch around the needle, join, and work in patterns as you did for the body. Or use different patterns if you wish. Mark one stitch for the underarm seam line, and increase one stitch each side of it every fourth round clear up to the top of the sleeve, keeping the increases in pattern. I like to make this seam stitch in the pattern color, but you don't have to. When I come to a round or rounds where the pattern color is not in use, I just slip the stitch and pull it up an extra round. A small cheat, and permissible.

There will be fewer patterns on the sleeve than on the body, but this is normal, as the sleeve is shorter. When it is the right length, cast off. Most ski sweater sleeves are around 17″-18″ long, i.e., shorter than you would think, because of the dropped shoulders. To be exact, ascertain the shirtsleeve-length of the wearer. This is taken from the middle of the back of the neck, round the elbow, to the wrist. Thus half the body-width, plus the length of the sleeve, should equal the shirtsleeve length, always allowing for a slight stretch in the knitted fabric. Overly long sleeves are a common error, and one I frequently commit myself.

Only when the sleeves are finished can you cut the armholes, as only then do you know exactly how deep to cut them. The tops of the sleeves started with 20% of body stitches, and increased at the rate of two stitches every four rounds, will be about half as wide as the body, which is as it should be for a nice easy fit.

Run a basting line down the exact sides of the upper half of the sweater, centering any large patterns, if possible, and seeing to it that the pattern-change line comes at the underarm. Now lay sweater and sleeve out flat. Measure, mark, and baste the underarm point on the body, so that the armholes match the exact width of the sleeve-top. It is most important that the armhole be neither longer nor shorter than the sleeve-top. Go to your (or your neighbor's) sewing machine, shorten the stitch to minimum, and stitch twice down either side of the basting and across the bottom, to hold each thread of wool in place and absolutely prevent its raveling. Keep the machine-stitched rows quite close together; we want neither to have a bulky seam nor to waste a square millimeter of our knitting. Cut on basting, then lie down in a darkened room for fifteen minutes to recover. You will never fear to cut again. (But always be sure to cut at the right place.)

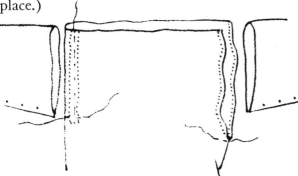

32. BASTED, STITCHED, AND CUT ARMHOLES

Join the shoulder seams, by sewing over and over, stitch for stitch, on the right side, or by weaving, whichever pleases you most. Shoulder seams should be very firmly joined. as their tendency to stretch is marked.

61

The cut armhole now thumbs its nose at you, having lengthened by at least an inch. You thumb your nose right back at it, because you *know* it was measured exactly, and that you are the one who is going to ease it to match the sleeve-top when you sew them together.

This is exactly what you do. Pin sleeve underarm to body underarm, and sleeve-top to shoulder seam, lapping the sleeve over the body. Put a pin at the half way mark, and one at the quarter, and then hem the sleeve neatly into place, from the right side, with wool to match it. Take one cast-off stitch from the sleeve and a piece of the armhole fabric alternately, about one stitch from the machine-stitching, seeing to it that the sewing is guided by the vertical line of the stitches on the body.

On the inside, with a steam iron, press the raw edges towards the sleeve, trim off any fuzz, and hold them in place with herring-bone stitch, or any whipping stitch, using thinner wool if you have any, or sewing-thread.

Hem the lower edges on body and sleeves (see p. 34).

If you prefer a ribbed edge, it is better to have started with ribbing. Casting-on is preferable at the lower edge to casting-off.

For neck-openings, the usual rule is to leave one-third of the top open; those with large heads may need a little more, those with small heads a little less. The main thing is that the neck pass easily over the head; all else is secondary to this. For babies and small children you may leave up to half the top open.

The resulting boat-shaped neck may be built up by knitting up all stitches on a 16″ needle, and working a stand-up crew neck or a turtle neck in ribbing. A crew neck may also be made in stocking stitch backed with a hem of a different color. At the desired height of the neck put in one round of purl to turn the hem and make it lie flat.

You may like the neckline just the way it is, in which case it is good to back it with a hem to prevent curling. Knit up all stitches, possibly in a different color, and preferably in a thinner wool. Work the hem in stocking stitch, increasing as sharply as possible on either side (increase 2 stitches *every* round), so that the hem will lie flat. After about 2″ pull out the needle, and sew the hem down. You may omit the increases in the last two rounds.

Lastly there is what I call the Norwegian neck, which raises the neck-back in a very satisfactory fashion. Knit up neck-back stitches only and work back and forth in garter stitch or ribbing for 1½-2″. Cast off. Sew the sides of this piece to the ends of the neck-front.

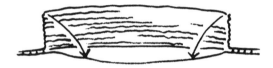

33. NORWEGIAN NECK

Oh yes; if you feel adventurous, you may make a kangaroo-pouch neck. (See p. 87.)

Chapter 4

Seamless Sweaters

My favorite sweater is the seamless one.

This was also designed when the children were little. As they grew out of the original ski sweaters they started agitating for yoke sweaters, which were then just coming into style. So I started knitting again with snowflakes on the bodies, and as I worked my way up, cogitated on the possibility of somehow uniting body and sleeves for the yoke, instead of knitting in patterns at the sleeve-tops to simulate a yoke. (Remember; this was years ago. The little girls are now grown-up married women.) I had seen sweaters knitted in one piece at the yoke, but they were frequently very tight at the underarm point, and tended to wear out there first. Suppose I cast off a few stitches at the underarms on body and sleeves, and sewed these cast-off pieces together afterwards? What did I have to lose? I cast them off, united body and sleeves on a 24″ circular needle, worked a row of rather banal hearts around the whole yoke, and departed on vacation, for some reason leaving the unfinished sweater in the local knit shop.

By the time I returned, three of the knit shop habituées were copying the sweater for themselves. It was up to me to finish the design. Perhaps this is why the patterns and the decreasings on this particular model were erratic, to say the least, because of all the scuffle and confusion. But they worked out adequately, and the sweater was copied, copied, and re-copied. I still meet up with it occasionally.

What inspired me to shape the back of the neck high and leave the front low I shall never know—no other knitted yokes to date incorporate this elementary piece of horse sense. Maybe it was Saint Paul the Hermit, patron Saint of weaving and perhaps also of knitting.

I shall always be grateful to two unknown ladies from another part of town, who popped into the knit shop one day, scouting around, as ladies will. They saw and admired the sweater, examined the underarms, murmured "Weaving?" one to another, and departed. All right; they were going to copy my sweater; I would pick up their weaving idea. Was this resourcefulness or just plain thievery? Anyway, I adopted the woven underarm as my own, and the seamless sweater was born. If you count woven underarms as a seam, then not entirely seamless. But weaving—or grafting, as the English so endearingly call it—works sheer magic and cannot be called a seam. It fuses two pieces of knitted fabric, and unites them undetectably; actually it comes into the sleight-of-hand category.

There are two great advantages to seamless sweaters. First, and most important, they are comfortable, as they will stretch in all directions. You can take your arm out of the sleeve, elbow first, without any ominous sounds of popping threads. Secondly, having no seams, they demand no sewing skills at all. After you have made your first one you will possibly discover another advantage; that of mindless manual activity, which, with a little practice, will leave your eyes free to read, observe the landscape, or glue themselves

65

to the tiny screen. So keep an open mind, and venture into the territory of the seamless sweater.

The four sweaters which follow are all seamless, and identical up to the underarms. If you diligently follow instructions when making the first one, the other three should be duck soup. All four may be made to your exact measurements, so refer to the notes on GAUGE, fabric, GAUGE, body-measurement, GAUGE, percentages, and GAUGE.

For babies' and small children's sweaters the same percentages may be followed, with one exception. Since young arms are pretty straight, I do not shape the sleeves, but start right out with 33% of body stitches on four needles, prefaced by a generous border of ribbing, to allow for growth.

The directions are chattily written, and I would strongly advise that you read them through at least once before casting on.

1. SEAMLESS YOKE SWEATER

Materials depend on your size and taste. If you are using knitting worsted (very advisable for beginners), five to six 4oz skeins are usually enough; in finer wool you will need less by weight. You would be well advised to consult the salesclerk. You will need a 16″ needle for the sleeves and neck, and a longer one (I prefer a 24″ one) for body and yoke. Needle size depends on the wool and on the way *you* knit; for knitting worsted anything between a size 5 and a size 8.

Decide on the width of your sweater. There is no set rule for this as bodies and tastes in fit vary enormously. Pay no attention to your "size," be it size 7, you enviable creature, or 54½. The important thing is the body-width *you* want, and the best way to ascertain this is to lay your favorite

66

sweater out flat, and measure it. Multiply the number of inches around by your GAUGE (see Chapter 2), and the result is the number of stitches to cast on for the sweater body. This is almost the only measuring and deciding you will have to do for yourself (after all, no one can do it for you), and it is important to do it accurately and conscientiously. Otherwise you may sup the porridge of regret with the spoon of sorrow.

From now on you may follow the percentages I have carefully worked out for you, deciding for yourself only how long your body and your sleeves will be. I can hardly do that for you. Don't worry about borders; they are added at the end.

On a 24″ circular needle, *cast on* the number of stitches

67

you have calculated. Let us assume that you have 200 stitches, which is a surprisingly usual number. Join, by knitting the first three stitches with both yarn ends, and *knit on up the body,* first being very careful to check that the cast-on stitches are not twisted on the needle. If, after working several inches, you find that you *do* have a twist, you may either rip the whole thing, or machine-stitch and slice your knitting vertically, continue, and end up with a cardigan or with a sweater with a small seam at the bottom of one side.

The body will be the major part of your project and may take some time to complete. Why not start a sleeve in the meantime? It will be quite a small piece of knitting, and can accompany you on trips, or live in its basket in the kitchen, waiting for any spare attention you can give it.

A long sleeve is started with one-fifth (20%) of the body-stitches; in the case of a 200-stitch sweater, 40 stitches. Cast them on on a 16″ needle, working very loosely, so that they reach around. (You may use four sock needles at the beginning of a sleeve if you wish.) Join, as for the body, and work around. After four rounds make your first increase:

Mark 3 stitches for the vertical underarm line, and increase one stitch before these three stitches and one after them (see p. 27). Work four more rounds and repeat these increases, using whatever method you prefer. I like to make a firm backward loop over my right needle (M1) for my increase, as this is a very invisible method, and is also independent of any other stitch. The main thing is that the three stitches of your underarm line remain undisturbed. They will soon start to be visible between the increases, and will serve as a guide to keep the increase-line straight.

Continue to increase every fifth round until you have ⅓ of your body stitches, or 33%. In the case of a 200-stitch sweater it will be between 66 and 67 stitches; let us say 66 stitches. From this point you will work straight to the underarm. Decide how long the sleeve is to be by trying it on, and stop knitting when you are about two inches shy of your actual underarm. Sleeves for the average adult are usually in the neighborhood of 18″ long.

For a ¾ sleeve, cast on ¼ of body-stitches, or 25%; in this case 50 stitches. Increase at the same rate of two stitches every fifth round. When you have 66 stitches, work straight to underarm.

Make a second sleeve, and by this time the body is possibly as long as you want it—anything between 12″ and 20″, depending on taste; *your* taste, remember.

Now the long haul is over, and the fun begins.

You are about to unite body and sleeves on one long needle. Some stitches will be left on threads at the underarms of body and of sleeves. The remaining stitches of body and sleeves will be combined to form the yoke.

For the underarms of the body you take 8% of the body stitches (in this case 16; 8% of 200). Put them on threads, 16 at either side of the body, so that there are the same number of stitches on front and on back. Be *sure* to have the underarms of the body-piece diametrically opposed.

On each sleeve, put on threads the 16 stitches which are directly above the underarm increase.

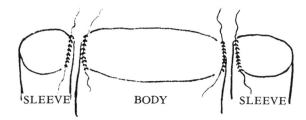

SLEEVE   BODY   SLEEVE

34. JOINING BODY AND SLEEVES

When the four blocks of 16 stitches are all on threads, unite all remaining stitches on the long needle, matching underarms, of course. Start working around with whichever ball of wool is most convenient, and break off the others.

On a yoke sweater, the distance between the point where you are now and the neck (exclusive of neck-shaping and border) is about ¼ of the circumference of the body—better a little more than a little less. Our sweater is 40″ around, so the yoke will be about 10″ deep. The first half of this— 5″—will be worked without any shaping, so here is your chance to put in any color patterns that take your fancy. If they are patterns with a wide repeat, see to it that they are centered, and that they fit into the number of stitches which you have on the yoke, which are:

200 body-stitches, less 2 x 16 for underarms....................168 sts
132 stitches on both sleeves, less 2 x 16 for underarms..<u>100</u> sts

in all   268 sts.

It is quite legal at this point to increase or decrease as many as five or six stitches, evenly-spaced, so that the pattern will fit in. The pattern I suggest is only 4 stitches wide, so it will fit in perfectly—67 times.

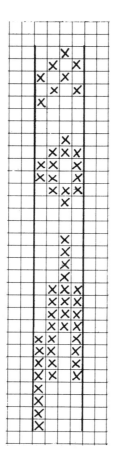

35. START HERE, REPEAT FROM ⊙

Work about 1″ plain before starting any patterns, for if these are placed too close to the underarm, they may become distorted. I like to start my pattern rounds behind the left shoulder. If you are planning a cardigan, you may change rounds at center-front, and then be sure to center the patterns.

Take care, when working color patterns, to carry your wool very l-o-o-s-e-l-y on the wrong side; it can hardly be too loose. Excessively loose threads may be (albeit laboriously) tightened later, but tight threads are beyond help. Try to avoid patterns which would have you carry your wool for more than five stitches.

When the yoke is roughly 5″ deep, it is time to decrease, or "narrow" it, as the old books say. This is achieved fast and brutally by working K1, K2 together, around, decreasing your total of 268 stitches by ⅓ to approximately 179 stitches. You will be working two more decrease rounds of this kind between now and the total yoke depth of 10″, so try to space these at about 7″ and 10″, contingent, of course, upon your patterns. After the second K1 K2 tog. decrease you will have about 120 stitches, and after the third about 80 stitches, which is right for the neck (40% of 200 stitches of body).

Between the decrease rounds put in any small patterns that attract you; the truth is that *anything* looks attractive here. Having successfully completed your first two or three yokes, you may well find yourself incorporating the decrease rounds into the actual patterns.

You can introduce colors in the design of your yoke to match any skirts or blouses in your wardrobe; it is surprising how effective this can be. One round of occasional orange stitches lies doggo until you put on an orange skirt, when it jumps to attention and hollers. (It is also quite possible to embroider a few rows in duplicate stitch on an old sweater-yoke, to go with the color of a newly acquired skirt.)

Naturally you don't have to put in any color patterns at all; a plain sweater is always pretty and suitable, and doesn't clash with a plaid or patterned skirt. The temptation, however, to put in at least one pattern is usually pretty strong.

When the yoke is about 10″ long, or one-half of body-width, and has been decreased to about 40% of the body stitches, i.e., about 80 stitches, we come to the most important part of the whole sweater—the *back-of-neck shaping*. This is worked as follows:

Let us take it that you have decided on a K1, P1, rib for the neck border. Starting at left shoulder, turn, and work back to right shoulder in K1, P1, for 40 stitches. Slip all first stitches. Turn. K1, P1, for 42 stitches. Turn. K1, P1, for 44 stitches. Turn. Continue working back and forth in this

71

fashion, taking on two more stitches at the end of each row, for a total of six rows (52 sts). When you arrive at what threatens to become a loose hole, as you will every time you pass a turn, pick up a stitch from under the stitch on the needle (see Illus. #24, p. 39), and work it together with the loose stitch. This maneuver will occur at the beginning of the ribbing, which will render it pretty invisible. After the six rows of back-and-forth ribbing, continue around for about 1″ of ribbing, and cast off fairly loosely, so that the head may pass freely through the neck opening. Run a doubled elastic thread through the inside of the neck edge, and adjust to fit.

The neck border may also be worked in garter stitch, or in K2, P2, ribbing, or in stocking stitch with a hem, through which you may run a piece of elastic.

Weave the underarms (see p. 29). Use a separate piece of wool, and not the threads already hanging there. This will facilitate the necessary small piece of fudging at each end of the weaving. This is the place where the knitted fabric comes together in a triangle, and it is hard to give a rule for finishing off. You must rely on a mixture of logic, instinct, and our old friend, resourcefulness.

Knit up all stitches around the lower edge, taking them from behind the row of cast-on stitches (see p. 35). Knit one round. Next round *K8, K2 together, repeat from * around (10% decrease). Work 1½″-2″, into which space you may fit a message. If the hem is made in much thinner wool, the 10% decrease becomes optional. Messages worked in the sweater wool stand out splendidly against a background of thinner wool.

Don't cast off, but baste hem flat, and sew down lightly, elastically, and invisibly. If you are really fussy, knit the last round of the hem in the sweater wool, and sew it down with the same wool—a very neat farewell to a good job of knitting.

Sleeves are finished in the same way for an adult's sweater; for a child's sweater you may want to have ribbing at the cuffs, to allow for growth.

2. SEAMLESS RAGLAN SWEATER

Follow directions for the yoke sweater (p. 66) to the point where all stitches are united on the long needle for the yoke (p. 69).

Work 1″-2″ plain, depending on whether you want a deepish armhole or not.

Now mark the four points where the body and the sleeves join. Place safety pins at these four points. Sleeve stitches must be absolutely equal (50 stitches each), and back and

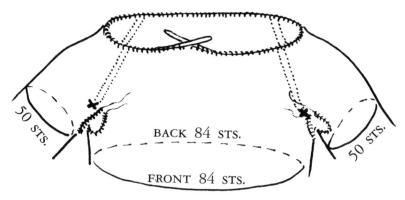

36.   ✗ = MARKERS, 2 ON FRONT, 2 ON BACK

front must also be equal (84 stitches each). Put safety pin markers *in* the 1st and the 84th stitches of back and of front. You will decrease 2 stitches at each of these four points every second round, as follows:

* Work to within 2 stitches of marked stitch, K2 together, K marked stitch, SSK (see p. 26). Repeat from * three more times (decrease-round completed; 8 stitches decreased). Work one round plain.

Continue working, alternating decrease-rounds and plain rounds. You will find yourself progressing like a house on fire, as the rounds will become shorter and shorter.

When 10 stitches remain of each sleeve section (not counting the decrease stitches), work the plain round and then shape neck-back as follows:

Place the stitches of the neck-front on a thread, with the exception of 5 stitches at each end (half of the 10 stitches of sleeves). Now work your decrease round as usual. When

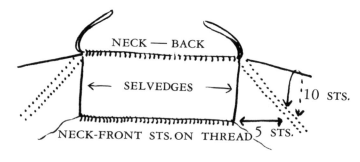

37. NECK-SHAPING

you come to the stitches on the thread, you will of course stop with a hiccup, as you can go no further. Turn, therefore, and purl back, instead of working the plain round. Turn, and work a decrease round. Turn, and purl back. Continue in this fashion until sleeve stitches and remaining neck-front stitches have been decreased out of existence.

The neck is now well and truly shaped, and all that remains to be done is to work around on all stitches for the border. When you come to the short pieces of selvedge at neck-sides, knit up about 5 stitches in each.

For borders and edges, see yoke sweater (p. 72).

The above neck-shaping figures apply to most adult raglan sweaters. With very thick wool you may care to start the shaping when only 8 sleeve stitches remain. With fine wool, such as Shetland or fingering, you may start the shaping when there are 12 or even 14 sleeve stitches.

Contrary to superstition, the *rate* of decrease for the shoulders is the same for any type of wool and any GAUGE.

3. SEAMLESS SADDLE-SHOULDERED SWEATER

A little more sophisticated, but worth the effort, really, and great fun to make.

Follow directions for the yoke sweater (p. 66) to the point where all stitches are united on the long needle for the yoke (p. 69).

Work 1″-2″ plain, depending on whether you want a deepish armhole or not.

Now measure your *own* shoulder-width in inches, and multiply this by your GAUGE. For the sake of argument, we will say that your shoulders measure 14″, which is average. Multiply this by your GAUGE of 5 stitches to 1″, and you will have 70 stitches. This is the key number.

Place safety pin markers in the first and last stitches of

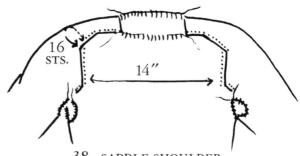

38. SADDLE-SHOULDER

front and of back. Sleeve stitches must be absolutely equal, and markers should be *in* the first and the 84th stitch.

Start decreasing one stitch at each of these four marked points *every* round, as follows:

Work across front stitches to within one stitch of marked stitch. *K2 together. Work across sleeve to marked stitch, SSK (or Sl1, K1, psso). Work across back to within one stitch of marked stitch, and repeat from *.

Continue thus, decreasing 4 stitches in each round, by these two methods, seeing to it that the marked stitches always consume the body stitches and not the sleeve stitches.

When the key number of 70 stitches remains on front and on back (including the marked stitches), change the direction of the decreasing to consume the sleeve instead of the body. You will thus be working SSK where you have been up to now working K 2 tog, and vice versa. Be sure to keep the marked stitches in line.

When 16 stitches of each sleeve remain, including the marked stitches, (8% of the 200 stitches of body), reverse the direction of the decreasing again, having the marked stitches consume the body instead of the sleeves. That is, where you have slipped one, knitted one, passed slipped stitch over (or SSK), knit two together instead. And vice versa. You only do this for ten rounds, but it is quite important, as it prevents your shoulders from becoming angular. It is also very visible, and one of the key-points of the design, so get it right. The marked stitches must consume first the body, then the sleeves, and then the body again, in a smooth flowing line.

When the ten rounds of this procedure are finished, make the first saddle, by working back and forth on one set of 16 stitches in stocking stitch—knit one row, purl one row, alternately. At the end of each knit row, slip the last stitch, knit one body stitch, and pass the slipped stitch over (or SSK). Turn. Purl 15 stitches to the end of the purl row, and purl the last stitch together with one body stitch. Turn. I like to slip all first stitches on this little piece.

After 16 rows of this, the saddle will have nibbled away in all about one quarter of the 70 stitches of the shoulder-width, or 18 stitches. Knit (or purl) your way across the remaining 42 stitches to the other shoulder, and repeat the process.

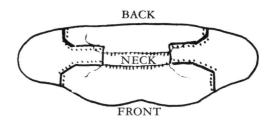

BACK

NECK

FRONT

39. BIRDSEYE VIEW OF SADDLE-SHOULDER

Enjoying yourself?

All right; now make a broad shallow "saddle" across the back of the neck for the all-important back-of-neck shaping. You have 34 stitches on the neck-back, right? Work back and forth on *them,* consuming one stitch of the saddles at the end of each row, as you did for the shoulders. When half (8 stitches) of each saddle remain, come up for air. Your sweater is done.

Make the neck border as for the yoke sweater (p. 72), and finish cuffs and lower edge in the same fashion.

4. SEAMLESS HYBRID SWEATER

I have only recently finished working on this design, so it has not been consumer-tested as the other three have been. (They are 10, 7, and 8 years old respectively.) So let us all hope for the best. It seems to fit all types of shoulders, and has a choice of two neck-backs, the second of which is a test of skill, indeed.

Follow directions for the yoke sweater (p. 66) to the point where all stitches are united on the long needle for the yoke (p. 69), except that only 10 stitches (5% of the 200 sts of body) are placed on threads at underarms on body and sleeves, and you have 292 stitches in all.

Start decreasing after only two rounds have been worked on all stitches. At each of the four joining-points of body and sleeves put a safety pin as marker into the edge stitches of body. Sleeve stitches must be absolutely equal, having 56

78

stitches each. Front and back must be equal too, with 90 stitches each.

Work to within one stitch of marked stitch, slip one, knit marked stitch and the following stitch together, pass slipped stitch over. You have decreased two stitches by uniting three stitches to form one, which in its turn becomes the marked stitch.

Conventional ring markers are nothing but a nuisance in a case like this (I never use them anyway); I can but recommend the common or garden safety pin. You needn't move it up every round unless you wish, and may soon find that you have left it far behind, as the pretty double decrease will serve as a marker in itself. Your left thumb will feel the

MARKED ST.

40. DOUBLE DECREASE

79

safety pin as you come to it, and will alert you to the fact that there may be a decrease coming up.

MARKED ST.

41. CHAIN DOUBLE-DECREASE

There is another very handsome double decrease that you may like to try: work to within one stitch of marked stitch, slip marked stitch and the one preceding it together as if to knit, knit the next stitch, pass both slipped stitches over it. This forms a very attractive chain running up the decrease line.

Work a decrease in whichever manner you prefer at all four armhole points. Then draw a deep breath and work two rounds plain. Be resolute in keeping the decreases always in an exact line, so that the marked stitch is always the center stitch of the next decrease.

Do you realize what is coming to pass? You are decreasing at a rate (8 stitches eliminated every third round) that is practically impossible to achieve except in circular knitting. Two-needle knitting is governed by the advisability of shaping every 2nd, 4th, or 6th row, etc., but circular knitting is bound by no such law. It allows you to decrease on even- or uneven-numbered rounds, depending upon the exigencies of your design. You *could* decrease 2 stitches every third row in two-needle knitting, but the directions might easily drive you—let alone me—up the wall.

The great advantage of this rate of decreasing is that it yields a most desirable shoulder-angle. Sometimes a regular raglan decrease gives you more of a right-angled armhole than you want, while decreasing at half the speed gives you a mournful bottleneck. Well, the above decrease of two stitches every third round gives you an angle in between, like the baby bear's bed, and it might turn out to be just what you want. Try it.

Keep repeating these three rounds, viz., one decrease round followed by two plain rounds, until 33 sleeve-stitches remain—one-half (50%) of the 66 stitches of upper arm.

80

Now make a saddle on these 33 stitches plus the two marked stitches; 35 stitches in all. Work back and forth on the 35 stitches for 44 rows. At the end of the knit rows, sl 1, K1, psso (or SSK); at the end of the purl rows, purl 2 together, each time nipping off one stitch from back or front respectively. Slip all first stitches. (In fact, the saddle is like that on the saddle-shouldered sweater, except that there are a few more stitches.) After 44 rows of saddle, knit or purl your way across 43 stitches to the other side and repeat. Then make a broad shallow saddle on the 21 stitches of the neck-back, working for 32 rows to eliminate 16 stitches from each saddle-shoulder. Finish neck and lower edges as on yoke sweater.

There is an even more intriguing way of finishing the back of the neck, and this is by making a *Shirt Yoke*.

After you have finished the first saddle, cast off the front half (16 stitches) of the 33 saddle stitches for side-neck. Keep working back and forth on the remaining 17 stitches, decreasing, of course, only at the end of the knit rows. This forms the shirt yoke, and you keep at it until 22 stitches remain on the back. Then make a saddle on the left shoulder, cast off 16 stitches for the other side-neck and weave the 17 remaining stitches to the 17 stitches of the shirt yoke. This is a bit tricky, as whichever way you slice it you will have half a stitch too many. But fudge this away somewhere

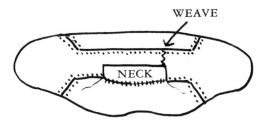

42. BIRDSEYE VIEW OF SHIRT-YOKE SHOULDER

with needle and wool, and I think you will find the result well worth the trouble.

A shoulder treatment like this may well exist in the annals of knitting, but if so, I have yet to encounter it.

Finish neck and lower edges as in yoke sweater (p. 71).

If you wish you may continue the shaping in neck-border as seen in illustration.

Any of these seamless sweaters may be made into a cardigan before the borders are added. Baste down exact center-front, machine-stitch twice each side of basting, using a very small machine-stitch, and cut on basting. Make borders as on p. 30.

May I add that one of the obliging characteristics of these four sweaters is that you can start them long before you have decided how you are going to end them; only after the underarm union do you have to make up your mind.

Chapter 5

Other Knitted Garments

1. KANGAROO-POUCH SWEATER

THIS design emerged in response to pleas for a circular sweater with set-in sleeves.

To create an appearance of set-in sleeves without actually sewing them in took some doing; I finally came up with the pouch technique. Here are directions for a 40″ sweater at a GAUGE of 5 sts to 1″. For every inch more or less that you want, add or subtract 5 stitches.

You will need 5-6 skeins of knitting worsted, or any wool which knits up at 5 sts to 1″, a 16″ and a 24″ circular needle, of a size to give *you* this GAUGE—somewhere between size 5 and size 8.

With the 24″ needle, *cast on* 200 stitches, or as many as your measurement and GAUGE indicate, join, and work straight to underarm.

Measure yourself from shoulder to shoulder, and multiply the inches by your GAUGE. Say the result is 70 stitches. Leaving 70 sts on your needle for front, and 70 sts for back, put the rest of the stitches on threads, exactly half on each side, for underarms. On the 200 st sweater this will be 30 sts on each side.

83

Cast on 2 stitches at each side, above the gaps, and continue working around as if nothing had happened—unnerving, with those pouches gaping at you from where the armholes should be, but they *are* the armholes, or at least part of them.

When you have worked about 7", or to shoulder height, cast off the front 72 stitches, and work back and forth on the back, eliminating 6 stitches at the beginning of each row by Mrs. Neumann's method (p. 25) until 24 stitches are left—about ⅓ of the back. Put these stitches on a thread. If you wish, you may put the center third of the front stitches on a thread too.

The body is done, and the fascinating armhole manoeuver begins. Baste down the exact sides of the top of the body to the pouch, right between those two cast-on stitches. With small machine-stitch, stitch twice each side of basting. Cut on basting. Sew the shoulders, taking a stitch from either side alternately, with the right side towards you. This makes a fine flat seam.

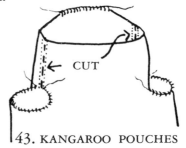

43. KANGAROO POUCHES

Take the pouch stitches of one side on the 16" circular needle, and knit up stitches around the cut portion of the armhole at the rate of two stitches for every three rows. You will end up with far too many stitches for a civilized armhole, but this has been foreseen, so keep calm. The problem will be turned into a distinct asset by working a sock heel for the sleeve-cap.

Hold on tight.

84

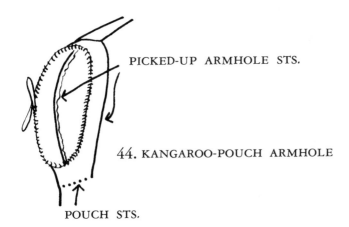

PICKED-UP ARMHOLE STS.

44. KANGAROO-POUCH ARMHOLE

POUCH STS.

First work around on all armhole stitches (about 90-100 of them) for about an inch, which will give the adventurous among you a fine chance to insert a small well-bred color pattern.

NOW; work to the top point of the sleeve, at the shoulder seam.

Row 1.   K5, SSK (or sl 1, K1, psso), K1, turn.

Row 2.   sl 1, P11, P2 tog, P1, turn.

Row 3.   sl 1, K12, SSK, K1, turn.

Row 4.   sl 1, P13, P2 tog, P1, turn.

Row 5.   sl 1, K14, SSK, K1, turn.

Row 6.   sl 1, P15, P2, tog, P1, turn

and so on. You are widening your sleeve cap by one stitch every row, and at the same time decreasing your armhole by one stitch every row. Involved? You bet; wait until you see the results.

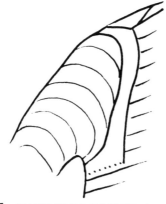

85

45. KANGAROO-POUCH SLEEVE

Keep a sharp eye on the total number of stitches on your needle. When they are down to 66 (33% of the 200 stitches of body), start working around on all 66, without further shaping, and *make a regular sleeve in reverse*. That is, work straight to the elbow (roughly 7"-8" from underarm), and then decrease 2 stitches every 5th round at the underarm until the sleeve is the right length—usually about 18" from underarm. End with a hem, or ribbing, or a band of garter stitch on 10% less stitches (K8, K2 together around), or whatever your heart desires. This is not quite as satisfactory a method of calculating exact wrist measurement as in a sleeve started at the lower edge—one runs into an element of uncertainty at the latter end, and sometimes a nice ribbed cuff is the best solution—you just have to take the bitter with

86

the batter, and you've got your set-in sleeve, haven't you?

Work the second sleeve, pick up stitches around the neck, and finish with a hemmed turtlish collar.

Having made one sweater of this type, you will doubtless wish to adventure with a *kangaroo-pouch neck.* Feel free. about 2″-3″ short of desired shoulder-height, put ⅓ of front stitches on a thread, and work to shoulder-height on this rather nightmarish object. Having cast off shoulder, slash armholes *and* neck. This is a quite valid way of shaping a neck-front. I sometimes use it on dropped-shouldered ski sweaters in preference to cutting out a piece and—shudder—throwing it away.

Finish lower edge with a hem or with a band of garter stitch on 10% less stitches. Start the sweater a few inches sooner if you want a mini-dress, but by the time this book falls into your hands such aberrations, it is to be hoped, will no longer be considered becoming. Becoming: a fine old-fashioned word in itself.

2. MODULAR TOMTEN JACKET

Tomten is the small Swedish elf who specializes in good deeds, and your child will resemble him strangely, if you put a Tomten jacket on him or her.

This versatile hooded sweater is worked in garter stitch, back and forth on two needles, and contains not one stitch of purl. Its only seams are the underarm sleeve seams.

Size, when using the directions given, will depend on the thickness of the wool used, and the resulting GAUGE.

With about three skeins of knitting worsted, at a GAUGE of 5 stitches to 1″, you will come up with a jacket for a child of 6 months and up, 22″ around.

Thicker wool at a GAUGE of 4 stitches to 1″, about 4 skeins of it, yields a jacket for a child of 2 years old and up, about 28″ around.

To make a jacket for a size 12 woman (37″ around), use about 6 skeins of very thick wool at a GAUGE of 3 sts to 1″.

For a small baby, take 4 ounces of baby wool, work at any GAUGE you feel like, and see what happens. Babies vary so much in size, and grow so fast, that the jacket will be gratefully worn at some period during the first year.

If for any reason you wish to have more or less stitches than those given, add or subtract them in multiples of eight, for the very good reason that this jacket is *modular*.

As the fabric is garter stitch, which seems to stretch in all directions, your sweater will grow with the wearer for a surprisingly long time.

Garter stitch is counted by ridges, each ridge consisting of two rows.

Cast on 112 stitches, as back and fronts are worked in one piece. Work straight for 40 ridges, long enough to reach a deep armhole. You may slip the first stitch of every row, or knit it, depending upon the school of thought to which you adhere. I slip all first stitches. Every seven ridges or so you may care to make a short row across the back, so that it will be somewhat longer than the fronts, and thus tend to ride up less. To do this, knit ¾ of the way across (84 sts), to R underarm, turn, knit 56 stitches to L underarm, turn, and continue knitting. This is a useful technique, and may be used with advantage on many plain sweaters. See p. 39 for the way to cope with any loose holes caused by turning.

At armhole height, divide the work as follows:

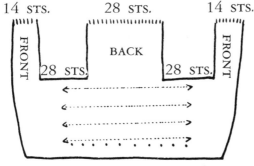

46. TOMTEN JACKET *(groundplan)*

Knit 14 stitches (⅛ of total) for right front, cast off 28 stitches (¼) for a very wide armhole, K 28 stitches for back, and cast off 28 for second armhole. Knit back and forth on the remaining 14 stitches for 28 ridges, to form a long skinny left front. Break wool, but do not cast off. Knit 28 ridges on right front, and on back. Assemble all 56 stitches of fronts and back on one needle, and work hood as follows: Increase 2 stitches at center-back every second row 7 times (70 sts). Work straight for 28 ridges, or desired length for hood. Knit to the middle of the row and weave sides together in garter stitch (see p. 29).

Now let's tackle those enormous armholes, which are deliberately made large, to fit over other sweaters, and to keep the child comfortable. Besides, they are good-looking, and contribute significantly to the styling of the sweater. Knit up one stitch for every ridge (two rows) by taking the knots at the ends of the ridges, several at a time, on a fine needle, and knitting them off with the regular needle. Knit up these stitches from the right side, using a contrasting color if you wish, for the first few rows, to accentuate the unusual armhole. There should be exactly 56 stitches for the 28 ridges on the front and the back armholes. Cheat, and add one more at the top of the shoulder (57 sts). Work straight for 4 ridges, and then start decreasing 2 stitches at the center of the row every fourth ridge. That's why I gave you that extra stitch; to make decreasing easier. Decrease 1 stitch each side of it.

When the sleeve is the right length—approximately 56 ridges—there should be around 28 stitches remaining. Cast off loosely, ending with a contrasting border if you wish. The sleeves should be a little long, if anything, so that cuffs may be turned back.

Is this not indeed a modular sweater? I love sevens, but it works equally well with any base number.

Sew the first 14 ridges of sleeve sides to the 14 stitches of lower armhole, and complete sleeve seams (see p. 28).

Sew in a jacket-zipper, by hand, from the right side, using matching thread. The strength of a zipper is in the zipper itself; it does *not* have to be machined in. Just take care that the ends are firmly attached.

This is the basic jacket. It has a few refinements which you may enjoy:
1. Start by casting on 10 fewer stitches (102). After 2″-3″ increase 10, evenly spaced, across back only.

2. Knit up one stitch for each ridge around the fronts and hood, and work a row or so of contrasting color. Cast off in purl on the right side.

3. For a hoodless jacket, decrease neck-back stitches at the rate of K1, K2 together before casting off, or before border. You may also scoop out neck-fronts if you wish. Include neck border with front border, mitering corners (see p. 31).

4. Line the hood by making a duplicate hood in thinner softer wool. Use a pretty pattern if your fancy dictates. Sew it into the hood proper. Make a cord (p. 104), thread it between hood and lining, attaching it at the top, and tie it under chin.

5. For a small baby, cords through cuff edges obviate the need for mittens.

6. Make a variation of the "Afterthought Pocket" (p. 37) by snipping one stitch at pocket center. Unravel in both directions as far as you wish. Pick up lower stitches and make a contrasting welt before casting off. You may also cast off immediately. Pick up upper stitches and work a square flap, to be sewn down lightly and invisibly inside.

7. A belt in the back can be added. Knit a small piece, horizontally or vertically, and attach with dummy buttons. Sew matching buttons under chin and add a loop.

8. For a coat, just make longer to underarm, and be sure to incorporate a few short rows across the back from side-seam to side-seam (see p. 89).

3. THIS BRINGS ME TO COATS
About which I have little to say.

They are just slightly larger, rather longer, sweaters.

Sports or casual coats, that is.

If you want a dressmaker coat, then you have to be somewhat of a dressmaker. As a knitter, I can be of little help to you here, except to enjoin you to study the knitting periodicals, which sometimes feature very dashing coats, indeed.

4. AND THIS BRINGS ME TO HATS

To which the sky is the limit. People will put *anything* on their heads, it seems to me for two reasons: either it keeps them warm, or it makes them feel cute. A good woolly cap can well combine these functions.

What is warmer or more becoming than a Watchcap? (They used to call them toques, and will, perhaps, again.)

A Tam-o'-Shanter is pulled forward over the eyes in a very jaunty manner when the sun shines; in a drizzle it may

be dragged down over the ears. It is also very useful for unexpected finds of mushrooms or blackberries.

A Snail-hat is the epitome of style and form in knitting, but can also be pulled over the ears in winter.

Caps are quickly made, and invaluable for using up scraps of wool for color patterns and stripes. They are excellent bazaar material, as people will pay more for them than for mittens, and they are quicker and more fun to make. (For me the great drawback to knitting mittens is that, having created one, you have to turn around and copy it exactly, for a pair.)

A basic rule for hats is that you start with 90-100 sts on a 16" circular needle with knitting worsted at a GAUGE of 5 sts to 1". This is a good starting rule, to be broken in all directions.

I *do* start with 90 stitches for a Tam-o'-Shanter, but almost immediately explode to 120 stitches or even more. For a Watchcap in the tricky and beautiful stitch, Prime Rib or Brioche Stitch, I start off with only 36 stitches, and stick to them.

So let us get down to some basic instructions, bearing in mind that one size fits all, subject to variations in taste.

Tam-o'-Shanter

You will need a 16" circular needle, and a set of four sock needles of approximately the same size for finishing

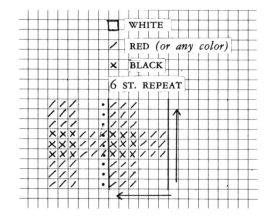

the top. Also some knitting worsted (GAUGE 5 sts to 1")
two to three ounces of it, or a pile of remnants. Needle
size will depend on how *you* knit—anything between a
size 5 and a size 8, for a GAUGE of 5 sts to 1".

Cast on 90 stitches on the circular needle. Join, being careful not to twist, and knit around for 10 rounds for the border
lining or hem. Purl one round. Knit 10 more rounds, and
here is your chance to put in something in the way of a pattern—perhaps a small Scottish-type check, such as is much
affected by the curling fraternity. And sorority, needless to
say.

Now increase suddenly to 120 sts, by working K3, M1
around. This is for an average tam; if you want a monster,
increase to 135 stitches by working K2, M1, around. And
so on; be limited only by your own desires. After 25 rounds
(about 3½") on 120 stitches, or 32 rounds (about 4½") on
135 stitches, start to decrease for the top. First get rid of one
or two stitches, as the case may be, so that there is a number of stitches divisible by seven—seven blocks of 17 or 19
stitches respectively. Decrease 7 stitches evenly spaced
around (K15, K2 tog, *or* K17, K2 tog, around), and then
work one plain round. Alternate these two rounds, decreasing seven by seven, until 49 stitches remain—nothing but
magic numbers. Now decrease every round (so that the tam
will not come to a point) until you are down to the last
seven stitches, which are fastened off. Naturally you will
have had the wit to change to the four needles when the
circular needle became unmanageable.

And what have you made? An old bag. Quite right; that's
all a tam is. You can forget all that elaborate increasing and
subsequent decreasing, and devote yourself to having a good
time with colors and patterns. Make regular stripes or ir-
regular ones. Introduce small color patterns, remembering

94

to keep the carried wool *very* loose. Set unexpected colors next to one another. Get carried away. (The vertical lines for a plaid tam are best put in later with a crochet hook.) You can have a wonderful time experimenting with a seven-pointed star in the latter reaches of the seven-pointed decreasing.

Now dampen your bag, get out one of the Thanksgiving Dinner plates, and stretch the tam over it, top side down. Pat the head-opening into shape, and leave to dry.

Tams have many variations. If you decrease by SSK, your star will swirl clockwise, if you decrease as above it will go widdershins. If you want a straight decrease, alternate these methods, or decrease two stitches at once, as for the shoulder of the Hybrid Sweater (p. 79) but only every fourth round.

A Two-Colored Hat (Gauge 5 sts to 1")
is made of about 4 oz of knitting worsted by casting on 91 sts, knitting to desired depth for head—about 6"— and decreasing in a 7-pointed star, as above. Knit up 91 stitches around the lower edge in a different color, and make a mirror-hat in the opposite direction. Push one hat inside the other, or, for variety, the other inside the one.

A Watchcap
is quick and easy, once you get the hang of the stitch.

You will need about 4 oz of very thick wool; thick enough to give a GAUGE of 2½ sts to 1" if worked in stocking stitch, and a pair of very thick needles, size 10½ to 15. The thicker the needles, the lighter and fluffier your watchcap.

The stitch is Prime Rib or Brioche Stitch, which gives many people grief, including knitting teachers, so listen carefully:

95

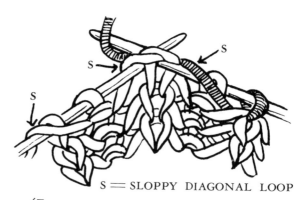

S = SLOPPY DIAGONAL LOOP

47. PRIME RIB OR BRIOCHE STITCH

Cast on 36 stitches. Work the first row *only once*. The pattern is formed by repeating row 2.

Row 1. *K1, bring wool forward to front of work, slip next stitch as if to purl, bring wool back *over* R needle, forming a sloppy diagonal loop. Repeat from *, ending yarn forward, slip one stitch as if to purl.

Row 2. K1, *yarn forward to front of work, slip next stitch as if to purl, bring wool back *over* R needle, forming sloppy diagonal loop, K2 together (the stitch and the sloppy diagonal loop from the previous row). Repeat from *, ending yarn forward, slip 1 st as if to purl.

That's it, and please excuse the wordiness. Prime Rib is written on my heart like Calais on Mary Tudor's.

This stitch is sometimes mistaken for Fisherman's Rib, where you knit into the stitch of the row below, but if you try them both on the same swatch, you will see that Prime Rib is well worth the trouble of learning, as it makes a much richer and fruitier rib. It is at its best worked quite loosely in very thick fluffy wool.

So take the fluffiest wool you can find, and a pair of enormous needles, and cast on 36 stitches, which will go easily around any head, such is the astonishing lateral stretch of this stitch. Work back and forth (Prime Rib is not suited to circular knitting) for from 7"-11", or even more—each individual has his or her favorite watchcap height—then decrease quite sharply by simply changing to ordinary K1,

P1, for four rows. On the next row, SSK across, which will eliminate the purl stitches. P 1 row, K 1 row, P 1 row. Next row, K2 together across, break wool, thread through the remaining 9 stitches, pull tight and secure. Weave sides cunningly together.

There; a lovely, practical, and versatile piece of headgear. Only one word of warning; it is virtually impossible to correct a mistake in Prime Rib, or even in Fisherman's Rib; you have to rip back to the error and pick up all the stitches again. So review your fabric closely after every row.

Snail Hat

The best part of Christmas is present-planning. Try some Snail Spiral Hats. They are interesting to make and inexpensive. Knit one in an evening. The largest available 16″ circular needle is #10½, so knit loosely.

GAUGE: 7½ sts. to 3″ measured over stocking stitch. MATE-RIALS: 1 skein Sheepsdown, 1 16″ circular needle #10½, 1 set of sock needles #10½. (If hard to find, sharpen single-pointed needles in the pencil-sharpener.) *Cast on* 50 sts. on a circular needle. K 5 rows back and forth. Next row (right side) increase by K2, M1 (making backward loop over R needle) around. (75 sts). Join and continue around. Now pay careful attention, as the spiral is about to start. *P2, P2 tog, K11, M1. Rep. from*. Keep repeating for 20 rounds. Pattern will edge to the left. Remember the M1, and count sts carefully until pattern is established. After 20 rounds, eliminate the M1. The stitches will become less and the hat starts coming to a point. At 35 sts. change to 4 needles. At 20 sts start slipping the remaining K st, knitting the next, and psso. At 5 sts fasten off. Sew border, and steam in a spiral. The model was designed for Sheepsdown, and there is no "just as good." This sounds commercial, but it is true. For a larger cap, work 25 rounds before starting to decrease.

97

A FEW REMARKS ON SOCKS

The best socks are made of wool. My husband once rescued a hunting dog from a half-frozen pond, and continued to hunt all day in soggy hip boots, his feet warm in soggy woolen socks. A pair of thick woolen socks has been likened to a pair of heating pads under the feet. Let synthetics try to make similar statements.

However, synthetics are extremely strong, so let us combine the virtues of both materials by incorporating a thin nylon thread in toes and heels.

I will make another downright statement: socks are best made on four needles. This dictum may intimidate the beginner, but once the technique is mastered, it becomes almost automatic. Work the first stitch on each needle quite tightly to prevent unsightly vertical looseness where the needles join, or you may carry 2 stitches forward as you finish each needle.

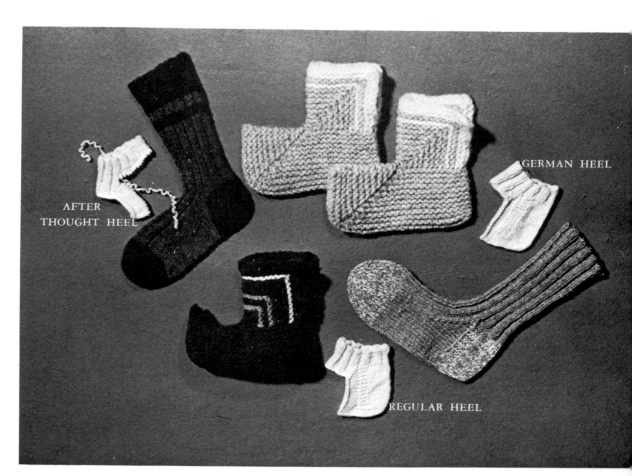

AFTER THOUGHT HEEL

GERMAN HEEL

REGULAR HEEL

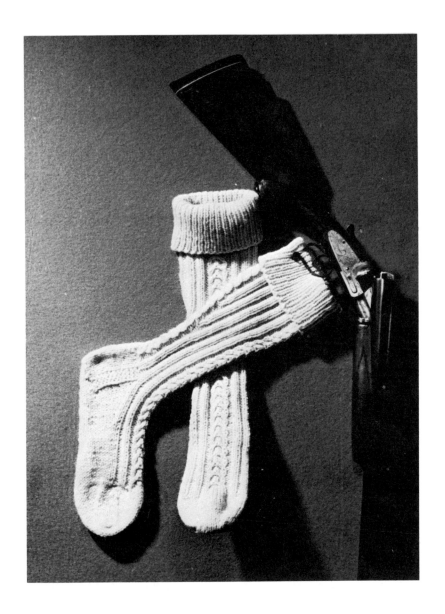

K2, P2, rib is one of the best stitches for socks, as it is so elastic that it clings to legs and ankles, and tends to stay up and not wrinkle. So cast on sufficient stitches to reach comfortably around ankle and/or instep, seeing to it that they are divisible by four, distribute them on three needles, and rib a long enough piece for the leg. Shaping for the calf is necessary only for stockings, although you may certainly shape a sock if you want to; it's rather fun.

The foot of a good sock should come out at a right angle,

99

the better to fit a right-angled foot, unless you are planning to wear hand-knitted socks with high-heeled shoes; something the fashion boys haven't thought of yet. The rule of thumb is to make the heel-flap on half of the stitches, and to have it as long as it is wide. So join in some fine nylon yarn, leave the front stitches in abeyance, and work back and forth in stocking stitch on the back half of the stitches until you have a square piece. I like to keep the sides of the heel-flap in garter stitch. That is, I knit the knit rows. On the purl rows, knit the first four and last four stitches. I also slip the first stitch, and purl the last one on each row, which gives a pretty and useful braided edge—a pleasure to knit up when the time comes.

When there are half as many garter stitch ridges as there are stitches on the heel-flap, I turn the heel.

These words may well strike terror into neophyte hearts. Try the following German method, which is very simple. When you have turned several heels in this fashion, you can graduate to the conventional method, which actually wears better.

German Heel

Say you have 30 stitches on your completed heel-flap. Knit $\frac{2}{3}$ of them (20 stitches), knitting the 20th stitch together with its left-hand neighbor. Turn. Purl $\frac{1}{3}$ of the stitches (10 stitches), purling the 10th stitch together with its left-hand neighbor. Turn. Work back and forth on these ten stitches, always working the last stitch together with one of the stitches from the end-pieces until the end-pieces are used up. I don't want to confuse you now, but after you have made one clean pair of heels in this way, you will see that it is better to purl two together on the purl row, and to

100

SSK at the end of the knit row. End up with the knit row, and cut the nylon thread.

Conventional Heel

When square heel-flap is completed, Knit to the halfway point.

SSK, (or sl 1, K1, psso), K1, turn.

P 2, P 2 tog, P 1, turn.

K 4, SSK, K 1, turn.

P 6, P 2 tog, P 1, turn, and so on, always decreasing at the gap caused by the previous turn. I like to slip all first stitches. When side-pieces are consumed, ending with a Knit row, continue as follows:

Knit up one stitch for each ridge along the side of the heel-flap, work those front stitches which have been patiently waiting since you began the heel, and knit up the stitches along the other side of the heel-flap.

Heel-turning completed. You may knit up both sides of the braid-like edge of the heel-flap, or just the back half, which looks very pretty and workmanlike.

At the point where the heel-flap joins the front stitches there is nearly always one loose stitch; don't ask me why. Knit into the back of it and it will disappear.

Ankle-shaping

Work on down the foot, decreasing away the surplus stitches at each ankle until you have the number of stitches you started with. You will find that by using both methods of decreasing—K2 together at the right side and SSK at the left side—you will attain a symmetrical decrease. You may decrease one stitch each side every row, every second row, or every third row. I prefer the happy medium.

The under part of the foot should be in stocking stitch—

101

what else?—but you may continue a panel of ribbing down the top of the foot to the big-toe joint, when it is time to join in the nylon thread again.

Shape for toe

Put half the stitches on one needle for sock-front, and a quarter on each of two other needles. The front needle is #2; the one before it #1; the one after it #3.

*On #1 needle, work to within 3 stitches of the end, K2 tog, K1. On #2 needle, K1, SSK, work to within 3 stitches of the end, K2 tog, K1. On #3 needle K1, SSK, knit to end. (4 stitches decreased.) Work one round plain. Rep from * until 20 stitches in all are left. Weave front to back.

When caught in the wilderness, knitting on socks, with no nylon thread available, I make the following heels:

Afterthought Heels

Knit a totally heelless sock as far as the big-toe joint, and keep making more of them until you get home. Then take nylon thread and finish off the toes. Snip one thread at the point where the top center of the heel-flap would be. Unravel the row of this stitch in either direction until you have a gaping hole ⅔ of the way around the sock with stitches waiting to be picked up above and below. Pick them up on three needles, with wool and nylon together, of course, work three rounds, and then make a toe, with the decrease points at the ankles. Try the sock on and you'll find that the second toe is actually a heel.

Some directions would have you perform this magic feat on only half the stitches instead of ⅔, but this makes rather a small heel, so that you may find wear occurring where the nylon *isn't*.

This heel is convenient for taking out and re-knitting, should it ever show signs of wear.

STOCKINGS

These have recently returned to favor with skiers, and very handsome they look, with their traditional black and white Norwegian designs. Small repeat patterns also look well, and I append a few here. Hikers and mountain climbers have never stopped wearing them, which shows their wisdom.

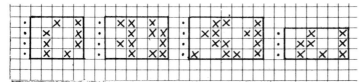

They are no more than long socks, except that you start with one-third more stitches. The distance between knee and ankle is usually about 12″, and is divided into thirds. The first third is worked straight, in the second third you decrease down to ankle measurement; the last third is worked straight. Then comes the foot, as described under SOCKS. The calf-decreasing can be fascinating. I sometimes make a small cable down the center-back, and work my decreasings in pairs, one on either side, about every 4-5 rounds, employing both decreasing methods.

A GOOD 2-NEEDLE GARTER STITCH
SLIPPER, WITH CUFF

You will need about 4oz of very thick wool (GAUGE 2½ sts to 1″), and a pair of thick needles, about size 11.

Cast on 51 stitches, and make angled cuff as follows:
Row 1.   K11, sl 1, K2 tog, psso, K23, sl 1, K2 tog, psso, K11.
Row 2, and all alternate rows, K.
Row 3.   K10, sl 1, K2 tog, psso, K21, sl 1, K2 tog, psso, K10.
Row 5.   K9, sl 1, K2 tog, psso, K19, sl 1, K2 tog, psso, K9.
Row 7.   K8, sl 1, K2 tog, psso, K17, sl 1, K2 tog, psso, K8.
Continue thus until you have 3 stitches left.

103

Pick up and knit 12 stitches along each side piece (27 sts).

Row 1. K12, M1, K1, M1, K1, M1, K1, M1, K12.

Row 2, and all alternate rows, K.

Row 3. K13, M1, K1, M1, K3, M1, K1, M1, K13.

Row 5. K14, M1, K1, M1, K5, M1, K1, M1, K14.

Row 7. K15, M1, K1, M1, K7, M1, K1, M1, K15.

Continue thus until you have 71 sts. Next row, K2 tog four times at beginning and end of row. Work to middle of next row and weave sides together (see garter stitch weaving, p. 29. Sew up heel. These boots come to an endearing point at the toe, so that you look like a Lapp, Eskimo, or Kurd. Work the same directions with baby wool and fine needles, and your baby will be the first on the block with different bootees. For a baby increase only to 51 sts, and work 4 rows straight before weaving sides together.

MITTENS

Aha! Many people's sole activity in the realm of knitting. To them I say skip this section. You are making the very best mittens, keep right on.

The following remarks are addressed to non-mitten-makers.

For children, make mittens with the thumbs sticking out at the sides so that they will fit either hand, and give them in trios, not in pairs. Joining a pair with a crocheted or twisted cord which runs through both coat-sleeves is a help too.

To make a twisted cord, take about 5 yards of wool, loop it around some outstanding object, as it might be a drawer-pull, knot the loose ends, and start twisting like mad. Certain types of beaters, or your husband's drill, will give you sufficient twisting in about 15 seconds, but experiment cautiously. Other types of beaters will become embedded in the wool as in a bird's nest, and you will wish you had never

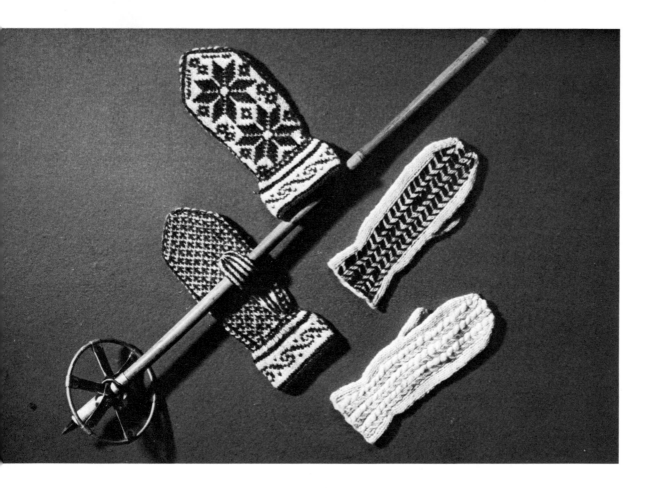

started. When the wool is sufficiently twisted, it will start counter-twisting into tight little loops, and this is the time to stop.

Take both ends—the looped end and the knotted one—and knot *them* together. Secure this knot by shutting the drawer on it, and pull out the resulting loop, which will be frantically trying to escape into many small loops. When you have tamed it, you will find that you have made a fine twisted cord, which I think looks better than a crocheted one, and which is certainly stronger.

Then there is Idiot's Delight: *an easy knitted cord*. Using a pair of double-pointed needles, cast on 3 sts. K3, slip the stitches to the other end of the needle, pull the wool firmly

105

across the back, and K3 again. Repeat until the cord is the right length. This actually makes a 3-stitch tube.

The thumb on a mitten does not demand elaborate increasing, although for many of us this is great fun, and very interesting. Thumb-shaping is avoided in the following directions, which are for a good basic mitten for an average woman's hand.

36-stitch Mittens

You will need 4 oz of knitting worsted, and a set of sock needles of a size to give *you* a GAUGE of 5 sts to 1″. If you want a GAUGE of 6 sts to 1″ for tough wind-and-weather-resistant mittens, increase the number of rows and stitches by 20% (one-fifth). But 5 sts to 1″ yields nice warm elastic mittens.

Cast on 36 stitches, and divide into 3—12 stitches on each of three needles. Join, and work around in a rib of K3, P1, for 10 rounds, or more if you want a long cuff. Next round, K2, SSK, around for a snug wrist (27 sts). Knit four rounds, and then increase up to 36 again by working K3, M1, around. Keep four of these increases in purl, if you wish, to run up the back of the hand, and work for 20 rounds. The sudden increase takes care of the thumb-widening quite nicely.

Now you are ready for the thumb itself, for which you prepare by the performance of a neat trick. With about 8″ of contrasting wool, knit 7 stitches where you want the thumb to start, which may be one or two stitches away from the first purl stitch. Put these 7 stitches back on the left needle, and continue working as if nothing had occurred, for 25 more rounds, or to the tip of the little finger.

Shape for the top as for a toe on a sock.

106

Let us now return to the tricky thumb. Pull out the 8″ of wool and you will find 13 stitches waiting to be picked up, 7 below and 6 above. Pick up the lower 7 on one needle. With another needle pick up the upper 6, as well as one extra stitch at each end, taken from the fabric of the knitting (8 sts). Take wool and the third needle and knit 5 of these 8 stitches. With the fourth needle knit the 3 remaining stitches (knitting into the back of the third one), plus 2 stitches from the lower needle. And there you are with 15 stitches neatly divided on three needles—just right for the thumb. (When you knitted into the back of that stitch you did away with one of those typical eyesores which like to appear each side of thumbs; the other one will be attended to when you finish off the wool where you started.) Knit 15 rounds on these 15 stitches, thread wool through all stitches, and fasten off.

I caused you to make those purl 1 ribs up the back as guidelines for optional embroidery. Work diagonal stitches with a blunt needle and contrasting wool, or, very subtly, with matching wool. See diagram. When you use the same color you can sometimes fool even experts into believing that you have used some esoteric and unknown knitting stitch.

48. EMBROIDERY FOR MITTENS

Scandinavian Mittens

These are an art in themselves. They usually have a great many stitches, and are *very* firmly knitted, which is a good thing, as some of the patterns demand that you carry the wool for a considerable number of stitches. The carried wool must then be twisted at the back of the work, and this tends to show on the right side unless the knitting is firm to the point of rigidity. This kind of mitten is practically wind- and waterproof—almost felt-like. Therefore it should

107

be relatively large for the wearer, as it will not stretch very much. Experiment with patterns, using large ones for the back, and small repeat-motifs for the palm. Divide these two areas—back and palm—by vertical stripes of the colors employed, and have a good time increasing for the thumb in pattern (2 stitches every 4th round). Border this area by a V of vertical stripes. The illustration shows a fairly loosely knitted mitten on 54 sts. at a GAUGE of 5½ stitches to 1″. The design demands only 8 twists.

Traditional colors are black and white, but there is no absolute obligation to keep to these.

SCARVES

They may be made back and forth on two needles, with as many stitches as you wish; the length is governed only by your patience and stamina. Since they are constantly being pulled lengthwise, make them wider than you deem necessary, as stretching them longer makes them narrower. Then, of course, the ends flare out. This offends me, personally, and I like to combat it by casting on fewer stitches (perhaps 10%, 15%?) than I need, and increasing up to par after two or three inches. The process is reversed at the latter end.

It is desirable to have scarves with no obvious right or wrong side, and this brings us to my favorite kind, which is a little more work, but, to me, well worth it.

Cast on 100 to 150 stitches on a 16″ circular needle, join, and work around until wool and endurance are almost exhausted. Then make a monstrous toe, decreasing 2 stitches on either side every second row until 50 stitches are left, which are woven together. To make a good rounded toe, decrease every second round to start with, and then every round. The beginning may be hemmed, and worn as a cap,

108

and the long end wrapped around your shoulders. It is quite possible to make a toe at the beginning too, by carefully un-ravelling the casting-on (or by starting with invisible cast-ing-on, p. 20), picking up the stitches, and working down in the other direction. You may still punch in one end and use it as a cap. It is a good idea to put in an occasional stripe, or a small Norwegian pattern, to show yourself that you are making progress, which is sometimes hard to believe.

The above scarf eliminates need for a fringe, which always seems a great waste of wool, and which usually becomes a bit draggled as time wears on. Do you know how to cope with a draggled fringe? When it is wet from washing, gather it up in a bunch in your hand, and slap it hard

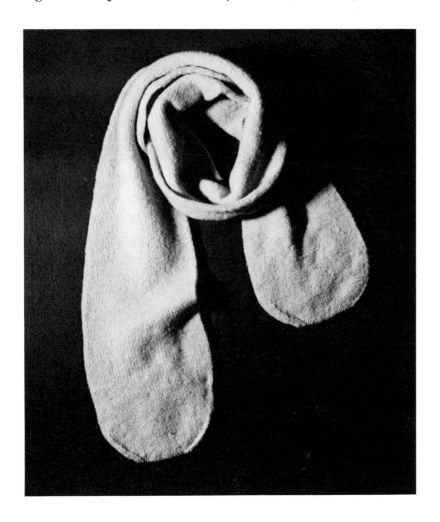

against an ironing board or kitchen table or other unyielding object. This works with any fringe, and saves much irritating work with a comb.

SKIRTS

I think I have covered the human (or feminine, anyhow) form in knitting with the exception of these. I make very few skirts, as, not having the figure to wear them without embarrassment, I am not too interested. But they are really very simple, being just a tube made on a circular needle, straight or flaring, as you wish.

The best plan is to start from the top, with generous waist measurement multiplied by your GAUGE, to give the number of stitches necessary. Take your widest body measurement—usually euphemistically referred to as hips—and multiply this also by your GAUGE. On you this spot is possibly about 7″ below your waistline, but in a knitted skirt you should increase to this width by about 4″, or, better still 3½″. From here on you may continue straight, or flared if you wish, to a length about 3″ shorter than you wish your skirt to be. Increases are most invisibly achieved by knitting into the *back* of the stitch of the row below (see p. 27).

Now hang your skirt up for a week, to settle.

When you take it down you will often find that it has settled into the length you want. If not, add or subtract a few rounds, ending with a scant 1″ of garter stitch on 10% less stitches. Or you may make a hem on 10% less stitches. Or you may crochet a border.

A skirt which is cast off at the lower edge is much easier to shorten (or, let us hope, one fine day, to lengthen), than one made in the opposite direction. Knitting may be comfortably ravelled only in the reverse direction to that in which it was knitted. A separated piece of stocking stitch or garter stitch may be continued up or down without ill effect, but this is *not* true of pattern stitches. They have to be continued in the original direction, or you will be half a stitch off.

SHAWLS, AFGHANS AND BLANKETS

To expatiate on the details of these would make a book far too fat, but don't neglect the possibilities of such warm, comfortable, practical, and eminently washable works of art —not to say heirlooms.

As they do not have to fit, GAUGE is not of vital importance. Neither is size; just keep on until you wish to stop. Dodge casting on and casting off as often as you can (see below). Employ fabrics which are the same on both sides, such as garter stitch, seed stitch, ribbing, basket weave, and glove stitch. Avoid stocking stitch and others which tend to curl at the edges. Unless you are a great stay-at-home, make afghans and blankets in relatively small pieces, which can travel around with you as you work on them, and be sewn together later.

Shawls

A beautiful feather-light shawl is the gift of gifts for a first baby. It may be inaugurated as the ceremonial wrap for coming home from the hospital; then it can grace the baptism with distinction. Later, it is eminently useful in imperceptibly keeping out draughts. Finally, packed away from danger in a plastic bag, it can await proms, graduations, and debuts. For a girl, that is. For a boy it had better become a linus right away.

Size is a matter of taste—anything from 30″ x 30″ on up is acceptable. Don't forget that a loosely knitted shawl, properly blocked, increases considerably in size.

111

To avoid cast-on edges as far as possible, I like to start my shawls in the middle, and have the increasings shape them to a square or a circle. Eight increased stitches every second round, 2 at each of four corners, will keep the shape square and flat. Sixteen increased stitches every fourth round at eight points will make it octagonal or round, depending on how it is blocked. This theory may be logically expanded to 32 stitches increased every eighth round, and so on ad infinitum, but don't start right away with such large figures, or the center will not lie flat.

There are two ways of avoiding a cast-off edge. One is to end up with a series of crocheted chain stitch loops which unite the knitted edge stitches in groups of three, four, or five with a single crochet.

I like to knit the border sideways in garter stitch. Work back and forth on a band of garter stitch, and instead of sewing it on later, work the last stitch of one side of it with one of the stitches of the last row of the shawl. You might think that this takes forever, but it doesn't. I have noticed that as a knitting project nears its final stitches, I come to love it more and more, and wish the end would never arrive. A long border helps me through this distressing period.

And why not hunt up some old knitted lace edging pattern and border your shawl with this? Generations may well wonder at your handiwork, preserve it reverently, and permit the newborn to wear it just for baptism.

Afghans
Their size, shape and texture depend on your personal taste, but they should not be too large, too square, or too heavy. We have a very useful one which is 44" x 72", but they may easily be smaller than this. They should be longer than wide, but how much longer is again a matter of taste; perhaps half as long again is a good rule of thumb. Knit

them loosely, in some lovely color to complement the room which they are to inhabit. Remember; they should be decorative as well as comforting.

Blankets

These are true heirlooms, and useful ones at that. They may be as heavy as you please, and their size is predicated on that of the bed, and on the amount of overhang you want. Make them in strips, or squares, or in any geometric shapes that will fit together conveniently. Consider some of the lovely squares for knitted cotton bedspreads, and imagine their possibilities in very thick, fairly loosely knitted wool. One of my favorite knitters has achieved a masterpiece of this kind, and added a two-purpose pillow-sham, which serves to keep warm the shoulders of a reader-in-bed.

The various pieces of afghans and blankets are best sewn together from the right side, taking a stitch from each side alternately. If practicable, use finer wool. When joining pieces of different colors, decide which color to use by tossing a coin; it's the only way.

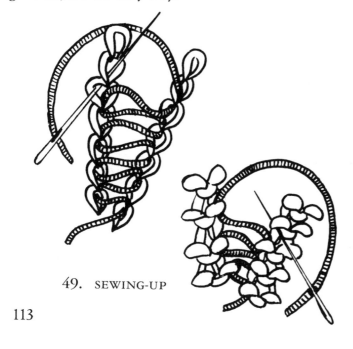

49. SEWING-UP

Chapter 6

The Washing of Sweaters

PLEASE refrain from sending your beautiful sweaters to be dry-cleaned, and sloshed about in the same fluid with heaven knows what.

They take time and care to make, so wash them with time and care.

The water—both suds and rinse water—should be 98.6° F., or baby's bath temperature. Thoroughly dissolve in this anything you trust; soap flakes, Woolite, special detergent for woolens, but not, perhaps, yellow laundry soap, although I have known this to be effective in competent hands. Lately I have been using shampoo, which seems to work as well as anything. But the main thing is the temperature of the water and rinse water.

Let your sweater lie in its soapy bath for a minute or two, to loosen the dirt, and then squeeze it gently a few times. If you have had the forethought to mark any particularly dirty spots with safety pins, these are easily found and attended to. Expel the soapy water by squeezing gently, but NEVER by wringing. I am the fortunate owner of an unautomatic, or thinking woman's wash-machine, so can use the spinning section of this. Rinse in water of the same tepid temperature, and then really get rid of every drop of rinse water.

When far from home and wash-machine I have been

known to sally into the out-of-doors with my dripping sweater in a salad basket, landing net, or pillowcase, and swing it round my head in an apparently lunatic fashion, to extract the water by centrifugal action, ending up by rolling it in several towels and even more loonily jumping on it. Anything to get rid of as much moisture as humanly possible, short of putting it in the drier. There is nothing more disheartening for a sweater than to lie in a sodden heap for any length of time. It can bring wicked thoughts of shrinking into its woolly little mind, as well as the idea of letting its colors run, just to spite you. Actually, contemporary wools are remarkably and wonderfully color-fast, but sometimes knitters are seduced by nameless bargain-wool, and then anything can happen.

All right then; you have a nice clean damp sweater, and a nice flat table, preferably covered with a large bath towel. All you need now are a pair of hands, a yardstick, and the confident knowledge that you are the master of your sweater. For you are. A damp sweater may be shaped to your will. It may even be made slightly larger or slightly smaller, by slightly stretching it, or gently coaxing it in.

First give it a good shake, to get rid of any uneven stitches. (Leave a cardigan buttoned up to start with.) Line up the underarm seams by the vertical lines of the stitches. If you have used my phoney underarm seams (p. 36), this will be quite easy.

Now; how many inches should it be around the chest? Use the yardstick and stretch or pat it to this measurement. On a woman's sweater pat the side seams straight up and down; for a man of heroic stature, taper in the lower edge. In either case, if there is a ribbed edge, coax it in and fold it upwards, to renew its elasticity. Fold up any ribbed cuffs, too. Pat the shoulders square or sloping, according to the shape of the wearer. Ease the neck-back up, and the neck-front down. This is particularly important in the sad case of those sweaters which have no neck shaping.

It is most important that the neck-back be at least 1" higher than the front—even on a crew neck. On a classic sweater the difference may be as much as 3". How often do you see people dragging the front of their sweaters down, because of feeling choked, and hiking the back up because their necks are cold? And what is the result? A sweater with a saggy front, and a pitiful gap between it and the pants behind. Remember; the neck-back of a well-fitting sweater should always be higher than the neck-front, and if it isn't, the least we can do is to block it higher.

The blocked cardigan may now be unbuttoned, and its edges lined up with the yardstick. Go away and do the breakfast dishes or something; the sweater will take some time to dry. Every time you pass through the room you can look at it with a fresh eye, and possibly amend your shaping, to make it look more and more like a real sweater. Don't take it up until it is bone dry. Then fold the sleeves across the chest, and turn the lower part of the body up over

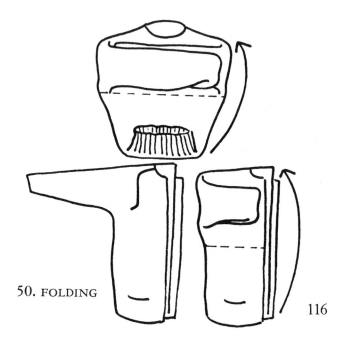

50. FOLDING

116

them, and there's your sweater, clean and sweet-smelling and folded, at practically no cost, and with very little expenditure of time.

If this is its last wash of the season, put it in a plastic bag with some of its friends, and secure the neck of the bag with several twangs of a rubber band or a twist 'em. Much better to be safe than sorry. And if you do suspect m . . . s in anything, isolate it in a plastic bag too, with mothballs, and examine it for damage outdoors.

I once had a sweater stretcher-drier, but abandoned it after two tries.

I have never tried making a brown paper pattern of a sweater when new, and blocking it to fit every time it's washed. I'm sure I'd lose the bits of brown paper.

And I have never succeeded in whitening a yellowed sweater.

Or in successfully stretching a shrunken one. I wonder if anybody can. I believe there is something in the construction of wool fibers which makes them *want* to stick together once they have been felted.

Sorry to end on this rather negative note, but "Truth is truth, though by an idiot, and spoke in error."

Let us try for a more positive envoi.

Knitting can be solace, inspiration, adventure. It is manual and mental therapy. It keeps us warm, as well as those we like and love. It has existed almost as long as the soft sheep, and in giving us wool they deprive themselves of no more than an uncomfortably warm fur coat in the heat of summer.

CAST OFF

Bibliography

Abbey, Barbara 101 WAYS TO IMPROVE YOUR KNITTING. Viking, New York, 1962.

Dillmont, Thérèse de ENCYCLOPEDIA OF NEEDLEWORK. D.M.C. Library, Mulhouse, France, 1880.

DICTIONARY OF KNITTING. Jardin des Modes, Paris, 1966.

GRAMMAIRE DE TRICOT. Jardin des Modes, Paris.

Kiewe, Heinz-Edgar CROSS-STITCH PATTERNS. Sebaldus Verlag, Nuremberg, 1960.

KNIT IT YOURSELF. Cappelens Forlag, Oslo, 1966.

Norbury, James TRADITIONAL KNITTING PATTERNS. Batsford, London, 1957.

Phillips, Mary Walker STEP BY STEP KNITTING. Golden Press, New York, 1967.

Sibbern-Bohn, Annchen NORWEGIAN KNITTING DESIGNS. Grondahl, Oslo, 1965.

STICKAT-MED TRADITION. LTS Förlag, Stockholm, 1965.

Thomas, Mary MARY THOMAS'S KNITTING BOOK. Hodder & Stoughton, London, 1938.

Thomas, Mary MARY THOMAS'S BOOK OF KNITTING PATTERNS. Hodder & Stoughton, London, 1943.

Walker, Barbara G. TREASURY OF KNITTING PATTERNS. Charles Scribner's Sons, New York, 1968.

Walker, Barbara G. SECOND TREASURY OF KNITTING PATTERNS. Charles Scribner's Sons, New York, 1970.

Williams, Susanne SCOTCH WOOL SHOP BOOK. Haverford, Pa., 1943.